PERSPECTIVES ON EARLY CHILDHOOD PSYCHOLOGY AND EDUCATION

SPECIAL FOCUS

Autism Spectrum Disorder

Volume 1, Issue 2
Fall 2016

ISBN: 978-0-9619518-9-4
ISSN: 2471-1527

Member

CELJ

Council of Editors of Learned Journals

PERSPECTIVES on EARLY CHILDHOOD PSYCHOLOGY and EDUCATION

TABLE OF CONTENTS

SPECIAL FOCUS:
AUTISM SPECTRUM DISORDER

Editor's Note

Welcome to the second issue of Volume 1 of *Perspectives on Early Childhood Psychology and Education*. The special focus in this issue is Autism Spectrum Disorder, guest edited by Susan M. Wilczynski and David E. McIntosh. Readers will find seven manuscripts on this topic plus an introduction to the special focus. In addition, there is one general manuscript addressing motor deficits in young children.

We are preparing the special focus for the spring 2017 issue that will be guest edited by Associate Editor Tammy Hughes. The topic is "Growing up poor: Negative sequelae on child development and beyond." Information regarding this special focus is found in the Call for Papers. We welcome manuscripts for this special focus and manuscripts that contribute to the general section of the issue.

Readers who are interested in becoming a member of the editorial board of *Perspectives* should contact me via email at PECPE@gonzaga.edu or alfonso@gonzaga.edu. In closing I hope you find *Perspectives* to be a useful journal in your research and practice. Please feel free to contact me with ideas, comments, and suggestions. We are very open to innovative ideas and look forward to hearing from you.

Enjoy *Perspectives*!

Vincent C. Alfonso, Ph.D.
Editor

Autism Spectrum Disorder

Introduction: Exploring the Need for a Multidisciplinary and Collaborative Approach to Treating Young Children with Autism Spectrum Disorder

Susan M. Wilczynski and David E. McIntosh

It is during the earliest years of life that symptoms of autism spectrum disorder (ASD) first come to the attention of parents, the educational system, and the community that connects with this population. ASD can have a profound effect not only on the child with ASD, but also on families, schools, and communities. For decades, professionals have worked to identify ASD at an earlier age. Early identification has been a central issue to researchers and practitioners because, ideally, effective treatment could close the gap between the skill sets of children with ASD and same-aged peers. If children with ASD can learn to talk, play, and develop self-care and early academic skills during this critical phase of development, it will be life changing for the child and his/her family, and it will be cost effective for schools and communities.

Much of the research on young children with ASD has rightly focused on early intensive behavioral intervention (EIBI), because this comprehensive approach to the treatment of ASD has yielded highly favorable outcomes. Despite the fact that research has consistently shown access to EIBI benefits a large percentage of the ASD population, researchers have many more questions they would like to see answered. Once treatment efficacy has been clearly established, researchers need to understand the parameters of effectiveness. For example, the contribution by Smith, Jordan, and Tiede (current issue) focuses on issues of generalizability to community settings, the factors that contribute to differences in treatment outcomes, and identification of treatment components that are needed to produce favorable outcomes. In addition, this article discusses alternatives to the EIBI model and how advances in technology are influencing treatment delivery. By exploring these issues, Smith et al. help the reader understand that although EIBI can be utterly life altering for many young children with ASD, researchers need to support practitioners by identifying factors that are essential for translating research to practice. This article serves as an example of what all approaches to treatment must do: Establish a research base and then ensure the outcomes can be meaningfully reproduced in real world settings.

Given the volume of evidence supporting early intensive behavioral interventions, families often seek these comprehensive programs for their young children. Parents typically begin their hunt for the right treatment program with an Internet search that can yield confusing and conflicting information. Zoder-Martell, Dieringer, LaBrie, Pistor, Duncan, and Gaither (current issue) describe the challenge parents face as they seek to determine whether or not a local EIBI program has effectively translated research into practice. They offer suggested information agencies should provide on their websites so that parents can expeditiously make informed decisions.

This special issue does not focus exclusively on EIBI, however. During the decades when EIBI endeavored to provide a broad range of answers to the autism community systematically, many additional concerns and treatment options were generated. This special issue is dedicated to the broadest range of issues that currently impact the autism community during the years of early childhood. Dieringer, Zoder-Martell, and Pistor (current issue) discuss the importance of gross motor needs of young children with ASD. Importantly, they address the considerable barriers to positive educational outcomes for young children with ASD when gross motor deficits are not sufficiently addressed. The gross motor needs of young children with ASD are often considered secondary or tertiary in comparison to the defining features of ASD. However, skill trajectories may be forever diminished if these gross motor skills are not sufficiently addressed. Finally, Dieringer et al. provide general suggestions for educators and caregivers of children with ASD to assist in developing and incorporating gross motor skills programming into existing early intervention programs.

Not all young children with ASD are served in traditional schools or in comprehensive EIBI treatment programs. Parents may not be able to access EIBI programs or they may feel there is not a good fit between these programs and their child's needs. Yet a two-fold challenge exists. First, young children with ASD clearly need access to efficacious treatments to improve their long-term outcomes. Second, alternative settings (e.g., daycare or Montessori schools) have unique cultures and resource constraints that may not support all efficacious treatments for ASD. Wilczynski, Trammel, Caugherty, Shellabarger, McIntosh, and Kaake (current issue) consider the challenge of identifying ways in which alternative early childhood settings can incorporate efficacious treatments without violating the basic values of the setting or ignoring real-world constraints.

Many young children with ASD face challenges in the area of social communication. Difficulties with communication during early childhood are associated not only with more limited opportunities to interact with others and to learn new skills but barriers to communication are often associated with significant behavior problems. Children who demonstrate serious behavior problems during early childhood are likely to experience more restricted environments as they proceed through their school years. Two procedures have emerged to produce significant improvements in communication during the early childhood years: Picture Exchange Communication System and Functional Communication Training. LaBelle, Jones, Charlop, and Thomas (current issue) demonstrate the effectiveness of combining these two approaches to produce stronger communication skills and reductions in problem behaviors. By effectively producing improvements in both areas, long-term outcomes for young children with ASD are likely to be optimized.

The final two articles in this special issue focus on how collaboration between professionals representing different disciplines and among a range of professionals with families can yield favorable outcomes for young children with ASD. McIntosh and Wilczynski (current issue) address the role registered nurses can play in meeting the healthcare needs of preschoolers with ASD. Children with ASD are often diagnosed with co-morbid conditions that complicate treatment decisions. Without coordination between professionals representing medical and behavioral disciplines, these children can be exposed to extensive assessment and intervention that are unwarranted and also reduce their exposure to effective treatments during a phase of development will set the trajectory for their long-term outcomes.

The last article in this special issue focuses on the importance of considering cultural variables when selecting treatments for young children with ASD. Evidence-based practice involves the use of professional judgment to combine the best available evidence about treatment efficacy with the values and preferences of clients. Wilczynski, Henderson, Harris, Kosmala, and Bostic (current issue) show how parents, as representatives of their children, can share culturally relevant factors that undermine or enhance the likely effectiveness of a given treatment. By reading their article, practitioners can learn how to incorporate the cultural values and preferences of clients and families into treatment selection more fully.

Together, the articles in this special issue demonstrate that the topic of ASD in early childhood is multifaceted and requires complex thinking on the part of practitioners. Not only do practitioners need to understand the evidence supporting different treatment options, but also, they need to understand how professionals representing diverse disciplines must work with parents to identify optimal treatments for each child. To establish an optimal trajectory for every young child with ASD, selecting treatments must involve knowledge about treatment efficacy, the unique needs of the child, and the perspective of the family whose daily lives are deeply influenced by the disorder.

Author's Note:

Correspondence concerning this article should be addressed to Susan M. Wilczynski, Ph.D., BCBA-D, Plassman Family Distinguished Professor, Ball State University, Department of Special Education, Muncie, IN 47306, Email: smwilczynski@bsu.edu.

Early Intensive Behavioral Intervention: Current Status of the UCLA Model and Future Directions

Tristram Smith, Allyson Jordan, and Gabrielle Tiede

Abstract

Early Intensive Behavioral Intervention (EIBI) is an efficacious, comprehensive, early intervention model for young children with autism spectrum disorder (ASD). The foundational EIBI model, developed by the UCLA Young Autism Project, aims to teach new skills to young children with ASD in a time-intensive, one-to-one format through discrete trial training. Research on this model has documented gains in IQ and adaptive behavior. Recent and ongoing studies aim to expand upon the knowledge base of EIBI by examining adaptations of the model in community settings, individual differences in outcomes, "active ingredients" in the model, alternatives to the UCLA EIBI model, and the integration of technology into intervention.

Key Words: autism spectrum disorder, early intervention, behavior analysis, behavior therapy

Much progress has been made toward identifying efficacious early intervention programs for preschool-age children with autism spectrum disorder (ASD; Interagency Autism Coordinating Committee, 2012). Notably, Early Intensive Behavioral Intervention (EIBI) begins before age 5, involves 20-40 hours per week of individualized treatment for two or more years, and appears to accelerate cognitive and academic growth in many of these children (Reichow, Barton, Boyd, & Hume, 2012). EIBI emphasizes highly structured, adult-led, one-to-one teaching approaches based on principles of operant conditioning and applied behavior analysis (ABA; Smith, 2011).

There is widespread agreement that, although children (and adults) with ASD have the potential to learn new skills throughout their lives, intervention during the toddler and preschool years is likely to have the largest impact because the children have not yet fallen as far behind and may be more amenable to change than older children with ASD (Myers & Johnson, 2007). Even in young children, however, intervention should generally be highly intensive in order to address the full scope of children's needs. Areas of difficulty may include the defining features of ASD (deficits in social communication and restricted or repetitive behaviors), as well as associated features, notably intellectual disability and challenging behaviors.

These considerations have led to the development of many different EIBI models (Handleman & Harris, 2001). Each of these models is comprehensive, aimed at helping children with ASD increase their functioning across domains and, ideally, catching up to their peers. All models also incorporate multiple ABA teaching methods, ranging from individual to large-group instruction, as well as formats that vary from highly structured and adult-led to play-based and child-led. Of these models, the best known and most studied is the approach developed at UCLA by Lovaas (1987) and colleagues. The remainder of this article reviews the UCLA/Lovaas model, its evidence base, current areas of research, and future directions.

Characteristics of the UCLA/Lovaas EIBI Model

In the UCLA model, most children start intervention when they are 3 years old or younger, although a few children begin a bit later, at 4-5 years old. Most have mild to moderate delays in development at intake, as indicated by IQ scores between 35 and 70, but children with higher or lower cognitive functioning may also be enrolled. The recommended dose involves 40 hours per week of one-to-one intervention for 2-3 years. However, fewer hours may be given to children younger than 3 years old, who often start with only 20 hours per week, and children approaching the end of intervention, for whom the number of treatment hours is progressively decreased (Smith, 2010).

To promote high-quality intervention, the UCLA model uses a hierarchical service-delivery model composed of four levels of providers: paraprofessionals, team leaders, case supervisors, and project directors (Smith 2010). Working in teams of 3-5 per case, paraprofessionals provide the majority of direct intervention, as well as attend clinic meetings with the child, parents, team leader, and case supervisor. Paraprofessionals are often undergraduates receiving college credit or paid research staff. Before providing intervention independently, new paraprofessionals must first work alongside a more experienced staff member (at least 25 hours) until observations of their performance by senior personnel demonstrate proficiency in implementing intervention procedures.

Paraprofessionals are directly supervised by a team leader, who has at least six months of experience in the UCLA model and has demonstrated procedural excellence. In addition to continuing to provide direct intervention, team leaders are responsible for coordinating the efforts of 2-4 teams of paraprofessionals. In turn, team leaders are managed by an experienced case supervisor, often a Board Certified Behavior Analyst at the master's or doctoral level. Finally, a master's or doctoral-level professional, with expertise in the UCLA Model and licensure in a mental health profession such as psychology, serves as the project director. Project directors coordinate frequent meetings among all levels of providers to promote effective communication regarding student progress and intervention plans. Additionally, project directors interact directly in intervention settings with therapists, families, and students to observe procedural fidelity first hand, and to solicit feedback from families and therapists regarding goals and progress. This system of oversight is intended to optimize coordination among providers by establishing clear responsibilities, expectations, and opportunities for feedback and communication.

Intervention is intended to maximize children's success and prevent failure. During the first year of treatment, most intervention occurs in the child's home, and discrete trial training (DTT) is the primary intervention technique. A discrete trial is a small unit of instruction (usually 5-20 seconds in duration) provided by an interventionist who works individually with a child with ASD in a distraction-free setting. The interventionist begins each trial with a clear and concise cue such as "Do this" or "What is it?" At the same time as the cue, or immediately following it, the interventionist may add a prompt such as pointing to or modeling the correct response if needed to help the child respond to the cue. Then the child has a few seconds to complete the response. If the response is accurate, the interventionist gives immediate reinforcement such as praise or an opportunity to play with a preferred toy. If the child makes an error, the interventionist corrects the error by saying "try again" (or something similar) or by showing the correct response. Finally, the interventionist pauses momentarily to separate the end of the learning trial from the beginning of the next, thus making each trial discrete from the others. This teaching format is designed to provide fast-paced, individualized, clear instruction, enabling the child to acquire new skills rapidly and experience mastery.

The first few months of intervention emphasize instruction on foundational skills that are considered prerequisites for learning other, more advanced skills. Examples of foundational skills include cooperation with simple directions, imitation, and discrimination between instructional stimuli (e.g., selecting a correct item from among a field of items, such as matching colors or pointing to objects or pictures presented by the examiner). At the same time, interventions are implemented to reduce behaviors that interfere with learning (e.g., tantrums or aggression) through behavioral procedures that are antecedent-based (e.g., re-arranging the environment), skill-based (e.g. learning appropriate replacement behaviors, such as making verbal requests instead of tantruming to gain access to a preferred activity), and consequence-based (e.g., extinction, time-out). Once a child has learned these foundational skills, the priority shifts to teaching skills that will improve the child's everyday functioning. Examples include communication skills such as requesting or labeling objects, daily living skills such as dressing, and play skills such as completing puzzles.

The second year focuses on increasing expressive and receptive language skills, including abstract language concepts (e.g., adjectives and other qualifiers, prepositions, pronouns), as well as generalizing new skills to preschool and other community settings. The third year emphasizes pre-academics such as early reading and writing skills, observational learning (learning by watching other children learn), and peer interaction. Also, as children spend increasing amounts of time in preschool or kindergarten, DTT is gradually reduced and replaced with more naturalistic instructional approaches.

Research on EIBI

In a pioneering study on the UCLA model of EIBI, Lovaas (1987) compared a group of 19 children with ASD who received this EIBI intervention to two less intensively treated comparison groups that contained 40 children with ASD. Children were assigned to EIBI if sufficient therapists were available at intake to provide EIBI; otherwise, the child entered a less intensive ABA group. Although the groups had similar IQs and behavioral profiles at intake, they had vastly different outcomes at age 7. The EIBI group had a mean IQ of 83, compared to mean IQs of 52 and 57 in the comparison groups. Nine children from the EIBI group (47%) achieved average intellectual functioning (IQ > 85) and unsupported placements in general education classrooms. Lovaas (1987) described these nine children as "normal functioning" and possibly even "recovered." A follow-up evaluation when children averaged 13 years of age (McEachin et al., 1993) indicated that children in the EIBI group maintained their IQ gains (measured by the Wechsler Intelligence Scale for Children) and demonstrated higher levels of adaptive behavior (measured by the Vineland Adaptive Behavior Scales) and lower levels of psychopathology (measured by the Personality Inventory for Children) than children in less intensive treatment programs.

The initial reports by Lovaas and colleagues were followed by more than 20 other studies on EIBI in the 1990s and 2000s. Two of these studies (Sallows & Graupner, 2005; Smith, Groen, & Wynn, 2000) improved on Lovaas's (1987) study by randomly assigning children to different intervention groups, instead of using a quasi-random assignment procedure such as basing assignments on therapist availability. Other studies used quasi-random assignment. Although many of these studies focused on the UCLA model (Cohen, Amerine-Dickens, & Smith, 2006; Eikeseth, Smith, Eldevik, & Jahr, 2002, 2007; Eldevik, Eikeseth, Jahr, & Smith, 2006), some centered on other EIBI approaches (e.g., Howard, Sparkman, Cohen, Green, & Stanislaw, 2005; Remington et al., 2007).

Since 2008, numerous systematic reviews and meta-analyses, using a wide range of methodologies, have evaluated the EIBI literature. Nearly all have concluded that EIBI is an efficacious intervention and that the UCLA model is the EIBI approach with the strongest support (Reichow, 2012). There have been varying estimates of how large the average benefits are. Reichow and Wolery (2009) calculated an effect size statistic (Cohen's d) of 0.69 for IQ, which indicates that the average child in EIBI attained a higher IQ than 75% of children who did not receive EIBI. These investigators also concluded that insufficient data were available to determine effect sizes for any outcome other than IQ. However, with some modifications to Reichow and Wolery's methodology, Eldevik et al. (2009) obtained an effect size of 1.10 for IQ and 0.66 for adaptive behavior, signifying that the average child in EIBI achieved a higher IQ than 90% of comparison children and a higher level of adaptive skills than 75% of comparison children. In this meta-analysis, comparison children were receiving no treatment, treatment-as-usual, or an eclectic treatment with similar intensity to EIBI (e.g., placement in community special education classrooms, speech services). Looking at individual differences among children who received EIBI, the same group of investigators (Eldevik et al., 2010) found that about 30% of children made reliable gains in IQ (beyond what could be attributed to random fluctuations in performance) and 20% made reliable gains in adaptive behavior.

While a consensus is emerging that EIBI is effective in increasing IQ and possibly adaptive behavior, many unanswered questions remain. Can EIBI be moved out of research settings and implemented successfully and sustainably over time in large, community-based programs? Can we identify the children who are most likely to benefit so that we can ensure they have access to EIBI? What are the "active ingredients" (Kasari, 2002)? For example, what is the best "dose" (amount of intervention)? What is the right mix of structured teaching methods such as DTT and more child-led interactions, and what skills are most important to teach? Although few firm answers are available to any of these questions, we review some emerging research in the next section.

EIBI in Community Settings

The favorable results of EIBI have heightened demand for this treatment. Many parts of the United States have passed legislation mandating insurance coverage of EIBI or other ABA interventions (Autism Speaks, 2013), and many publicly funded early intervention and preschool programs also offer EIBI (Simpson, Mundscheck, & Heflin, 2011). However, most EIBI studies have taken place at universities or specialized centers rather than community agencies. Therefore, it is essential to determine whether comparable outcomes can be obtained in community-based EIBI and whether these outcomes justify the substantial resources needed to achieve them. In the absence of this information, widespread implementation of EIBI may be premature (Al-Qabandi, Gorter, & Rosenbaum, 2011).

The available evidence indicates that community-based EIBI may be effective if closely supervised by experts in this intervention

(Cohen, Amerine-Dickens, & Smith, 2006; Eikeseth, Hayward, Gale, Gitlesen, & Eldevik, 2009; Remington et al., 2007), but that without this expertise outcomes are not as favorable (Bibby et al., 2001; Magiati, Charman, & Howlin, 2007). However, this evidence mainly consists of comparisons across studies, which differ not only in the amount of supervision but also in other important respects such as characteristics of the children and families who participated. Thus, it is uncertain whether the differences across studies reflect the differences in amount of supervision or other factors. In the only report that directly compared varying amounts of supervision received by children within the same study (Eikeseth et al., 2009), amount of supervision correlated with outcome, but the directionality of this correlation was unclear. For example, supervision may have been responsible for child improvements, or rapid child progress or high family motivation may have led to increases in the amount of supervision.

With few exceptions (Eikeseth, Klintwall, Jahr, & Karlsson, 2012), research on community-based EIBI has involved small agencies rather than public school systems, which are the largest service providers for children with ASD. Thus, research on implementation of EIBI by educators in public schools is a top priority (Kasari & Smith, 2013). This research may require collaboration with educators to adapt EIBI to fit school environments (Parsons et al., 2013). For example, children with ASD in public schools tend to have more advanced skills than children in most EIBI studies, almost all of whom show severe delays in intellectual and language functioning prior to intervention (Reichow, 2012). Perhaps because of such misalignment, educators often implement EIBI procedures inconsistently (Eikeseth et al., 2012). EIBI curricula may require revision to improve fidelity of implementation in public schools.

Although EIBI is expensive, it could be cost-effective in the long run if it reduces children's subsequent need for treatment (Jacobson, Mulick, & Green, 1998), as highlighted in a study focusing on an early intervention program that blends ABA and other approaches (the Early Start Denver model, discussed later in this article; Mandell, 2013). Children in this study were randomly assigned to receive either the Early Start Denver Model (ESDM) or community services as usual. During the four years after completing treatment, the 21 children who had been in ESDM received about one-third less treatment than did the 18 children who had been in community services--a substantial savings. Additional research is needed to replicate these findings and extend them to other EIBI approaches, but the findings provide encouraging initial evidence of cost-effectiveness.

Individual Differences in Outcome

Despite the overall positive findings on EIBI, studies consistently show large variations in outcomes across children. Some children with ASD (approximately 30%, according to a meta-analysis by Eldevik et al., 2010) can be considered "rapid learners" (Sallows & Graupner, 2005) who make large gains in IQ and other standardized tests and may catch up to their peers cognitively and academically. Most of the rest have been described as "moderate learners" (Sallows & Graupner, 2005) who acquire many new skills but do not catch up to their peers. Another group of perhaps 10-20% of children with ASD shows little or no improvement with this therapy (Lovaas, 1987; Smith et al., 2000). Given such a wide range of outcomes, it is essential to determine which children are most likely to derive maximum benefit from EIBI and increase access to EIBI for these children, while also investigating enhancements to EIBI or other treatment options for children who do not respond favorably.

The most consistent finding thus far is that higher pretreatment IQ predicts better outcomes. However, this prediction is far from perfect (Eldevik et al., 2009), as many children with low IQs do quite well, and some children with high IQs make little progress. Younger age has also predicted better outcome in some studies (e.g., Granpeesheh, Dixon, Tarbox, Kaplan, & Wilke, 2009), although this association is even less reliable than the link between IQ and outcome (Eldevik et al., 2009). Social engagement- including making requests, shifting gaze between an interesting toy and an adult, and imitating adult actions - may also predict better response (Smith, Klorman, & Mruzek, 2015). Similarly, a proclivity to socially-mediated reinforcers such as praise, rather than automatic reinforcers such as sensory feedback from manipulating an object, may be an asset in EIBI (Klintwall & Eikeseth, 2011). Interest in toys and the ability to echo others' speech may be a sign that children can learn from less structured teaching methods than DTT (Sherer & Schreibman, 2005). Randomized clinical trails (RCTs) are underway to determine which of these variables are related specifically to EIBI response and which predict a favorable outcome regardless of treatment (Rogers, n.d.). Also, cutting-edge RCTs are now starting to test whether non-responders can be identified early in treatment and whether intervention can be adapted to improve results for these children (Kasari, Smith, Kaiser, & Lord, n.d.). This research is a step towards making it possible to customize treatment in the future.

Active Ingredients of Intervention

In addition to child factors, particular components of EIBI are likely to be "active ingredients" that produce favorable outcomes (Kasari, 2002). Examples of possible active ingredients include the amount and kind of supervision, number of hours of EIBI ("dose"), level of parent engagement, and content and method of instruction. As previously noted, amount of supervision may be linked to outcome, although the evidence is only preliminary. Dose could also be important. Lovaas (1987) strongly recommended up to 40 hours per week of intervention so that children with ASD have the same learning opportunities as do typically developing children, who learn continuously throughout their day. Consistent with Lovaas's view, studies in which children received more than 30 hours per week of treatment have tended to report larger gains than studies in which children received fewer hours (Eldevik et al., 2009). However, following Lovaas's (1987) early comparison of EIBI and minimal treatment, only two reports have compared different doses for children within the same study. A study of 11 children with ASD did not show a connection between dose and outcome (Sheinkopf & Siegel, 1998), but a larger study involving 245 children with ASD, did indicate that higher dose correlated with better outcome (Granpeesheh et al., 2009). Thus, the evidence for dose as an active ingredient is suggestive but inconclusive.

Parental involvement is considered a crucial element in EIBI (Smith, 2010). Because parents know their child best, they have an integral role in treatment planning. Further, they are uniquely positioned to help generalize and extend gains made during EIBI sessions (Smith, 2010), which is vital because children with ASD have difficulty generalizing on their own. Studies indicate that parents can direct EIBI programs quite successfully with support from skilled EIBI supervisors (Sallows & Graupner, 2005). Preliminary evidence also indicates that consistent parent involvement can augment therapist-provided intervention and improve child outcomes (Strauss et al., 2012). Ongoing RCTs are examining the role of parental involvement more closely (Kasari, Smith, Lord, & Kaiser, n.d.; Kasari, Smith, & Landa, n.d.).

Much controversy has surrounded the method and content of EIBI instruction. The UCLA/Lovaas model emphasizes highly structured teaching formats, especially DTT. Conversely, many have suggested that embedding instruction in child-led, play-based interactions would be more effective because such interactions more closely resemble how children naturally learn language (Prizant & Wetherby, 2005). Despite such assertions, comparisons of EIBI programs that emphasize different methods of instruction are currently unavailable. Regarding content, most current EIBI programs aim to accelerate skill acquisition across all areas of development (the goal of most current EIBI programs), but some investigators have sought to streamline the intervention by specifically targeting core deficits of ASD, such as joint attention or symbolic play (Lovaas & Smith, 2003). Nevertheless, comparisons of EIBI programs with differing content have not yet been reported.

New Directions in EIBI Research

Alternative Models: Comprehensive Approaches

For many years, almost all EIBI research focused on the UCLA model or similar approaches (Smith, 2011). Recently, however, other EIBI models have garnered initial empirical support. Notably, the Early Start Denver Model (ESDM) combines child-led, play-based interactions to promote social communication with ABA strategies to teach specific skills in the context of these interactions. A well-designed RCT of 48 preschoolers with ASD indicated that ESDM, involving 25 hours per week of one-to-one instruction over two years, diminished ASD symptoms and accelerated cognitive development (Dawson et al., 2010). It also normalized how the children responded to faces, as measured by electroencephalogram recordings (Dawson et al., 2010). Moreover, as previously mentioned, ESDM was found to be cost effective, reducing the amount of services that children received after completing ESDM (Mandell et al., 2013). These results must be regarded as preliminary, pending replication by independent investigators, but they are highly promising.

LEAP (Learning Experiences and Alternative Program for Preschoolers) is an ABA intervention that is implemented in a classroom setting, rather than one-to-one instruction. The program emphasizes taking advantage of naturally occurring learning opportunities, using socially-mediated reinforcement, and coaching typically developing peers to model socially appropriate interactions (Strain & Bovey, 2011). A large, well-designed RCT of 294 preschoolers in 56 classrooms revealed that, after two years of intervention for 15 hours per week, children in LEAP classrooms improved more than children in comparison classrooms on measures of cognition, language, social skills, problem behavior, and autism symptoms (Strain & Bovey, 2011). However, a quasi-experimental study of 198 preschoolers with ASD in 75 classrooms found few differences in outcome among children in LEAP classrooms, children in another classroom model called TEACCH (Treatment and Education of Autistic and Related Communication-Handicapped Children), and community services as usual (Boyd et al., 2014). Possible reasons for the discrepant findings are that the groups in Boyd et al.'s (2014) study had pre-existing differences and that there was less quality assurance than in Strain and Bovey's (2011) study. Further research will be important in elucidating the effects of LEAP.

Now that empirical support is emerging for a variety of treatment models, a logical next step is to perform comparative effective studies to identify what treatments work best for achieving which outcome, and for whom. One ongoing RCT compares ESDM with the UCLA model of EIBI (Rogers, n.d.). Two other RCTs contrast a specific component of child-led interventions (i.e., sessions in which an adult and child interact during play), with a highly structured, adult-led format (i.e., DTT), which is a key component of the UCLA model (Kasari, Smith, Kaiser, & Lord, n.d.; Kasari, Smith, & Landa, n.d.).

Alternative Models: Focused Approaches

In addition to the aforementioned comprehensive treatment models, investigators are developing more focused treatments (i.e., treatments that target a specific outcome instead of addressing all areas of need). One focused treatment is Joint Attention, Symbolic Play, Engagement, and Regulation or JASPER. This approach aims to increase joint attention and functional play skills and spoken language by engaging children in reciprocal interactions with an interventionist within the context of preferred play activities. A study of 56 preschoolers with ASD indicated that 10-15 hours of intervention by a clinician, centering on either joint attention or symbolic play, increased joint attention, functional play, and spoken language skills as compared to children in a control group

(Kasari, Freeman, & Paparella, 2006) and that these gains remained evident in follow-ups conducted one year and five years later (Kasari, Gulsrud, Freeman, Paparella, & Hellemann, 2012; Kasari, Paparella, Freeman, & Jahromi, 2008). Recently, Kasari and colleagues have begun to evaluate whether teachers can implement JASPER effectively, with promising initial results (Goods, Ishijima, Chang, Kasari, 2013). They have also sought to integrate JASPER with a naturalistic, conversation-based language intervention, Enhanced Milieu Teaching (EMT) that provides direct instruction to expand children's spontaneous spoken communication during naturally occurring, child-led interactions (Kaiser & Hester, 1994; Kaiser, Yoder, & Keetz, 1992). Preliminary findings indicate that JASP-EMT has the potential to be an effective intervention for children with ASD who have little or no spoken language (Kasari et al., 2013).

Parent implementation of these strategies, however, has had more modest benefits on social communication (Oono, Honey, & McConachie, 2013). Greater success has been reported in a parent-based intervention that consists of 10-12 outpatient sessions with the goal of reducing children's disruptive behavior such as noncompliance or tantrums (Bearss et al., 2015). Efforts are currently underway to adapt this approach to other problem behaviors such as difficulties with feeding, sleep, or toileting (http://www.rubinetwork.org/research/ongoing-studies/).

Technology

Technological advances are influencing EIBI, particularly in the area of augmentative and alternative communication (AAC) for children with ASD who have little or no spoken language. In the 1970s and 1980s, the primary AAC system was sign language (Layton et al., 1988; Lovaas et al., 1981). Subsequently, with the increased availability of computer software to generate and print individualized materials, the use of picture symbols for AAC became widespread. Perhaps the most popular and extensively studied approach is the Picture Exchange Communication System (PECS), in which children learn to select a picture symbol and hand it to a listener as a means of communication (Frost & Bondy, 2002). Such systems often can be learned more quickly than sign language and are more likely to be understood by untrained individuals in children's everyday environments (Frost & Bondy, 2002). Though these systems do not always enable children to acquire spoken language, they are effective in establishing valuable communication skills in children who are otherwise nonverbal (Maglione, Gans, Das, Timbie, & Kasari, 2012) and have become a standard component of EIBI (Bondy & Frost, 2003).

More recently, computerized speech output devices have attracted attention. Devices such as a Dynavox™ may be smaller and more portable than a PECS book, and they can readily be programmed to arrange picture symbols in ways that meet the evolving needs of individual users. Commercially available tablets such as the Apple iPad also can be used as speech output devices with the purchase of software such as Proloquo2Go (Proloquo2Go, 2013). Such tablets are more compact, less costly, easier to purchase, and more broadly accepted than other communication devices and are increasingly considered a mainstay in the lives of children with ASD and their parents. They are one of the first devices originally intended for mainstream use to be adapted for use with special needs populations, including children with ASD (Shane et al., 2012).

Recent research indicates that children with ASD can use tablets for requesting in much the same way as they would use a picture exchange program (Flores et al., 2012). Children with ASD also can learn to use tablets for social communication such as commenting or conversing (Kasari et al., 2014). Researchers are currently exploring other possible uses, such as presenting videos of models demonstrating skills (Shane et al., 2012). Thus, tablets that were initially developed to facilitate cross-global communication now have the potential to help children with ASD connect to the world around them.

Conclusions and Future Directions

Lovaas's (1987) groundbreaking work on EIBI revolutionized the field of ASD intervention, and in the ensuing years researchers have confirmed his finding that EIBI can help some children with ASD catch up to their peers. Expanding upon his work, they have advanced the field in several key ways. First, they have built on Lovaas's initial model by providing evidence that EIBI can be implemented effectively and sustainably in community settings, although additional research is still needed to examine long-term sustainability and feasibility, particularly once the support of research staff is withdrawn. Second, studies have shown that child factors such as joint engagement and interest in social reinforcement, as well as intervention factors such as amount of supervision, may predict favorable response to EIBI. The eventual goal of these studies is to inform clinical practice by identifying child and intervention characteristics that predict success with different intervention approaches, providing an empirical basis for individualizing intervention. Third, studies on alternative intervention models and on the integration of new communication technology into EIBI have the potential to expand the number of viable intervention approaches and improve outcomes. Taken together, these advances provide grounds for optimism that EIBI will become increasingly available to the EIBI community and will evolve into an even more effective intervention. A relatively unexplored topic, however, is whether gains made as a result of EIBI persist over time. Evidence of long-term benefits would bolster arguments for widespread implementation.

Author's Note:

Correspondence concerning this article should be addressed to Dr. Tristram Smith, Division of Neurodevelopmental and Behavioral Pediatrics, Department of Pediatrics, Saunders Research Building, University of Rochester Medical Center, 265 Crittenden Blvd., Rochester, NY 14620. Email: Tristram_Smith@URMC.Rochester.edu. Telephone: (585) 273-351.

References

Al-Qabandi, M., Gorter, J. W., & Rosenbaum, P. (2011). Early autism detection: Are we ready for routine screening? *Pediatrics, 128*, 211-217.

Autism Speaks (2013). *Welcome #34! Oregon Enacts Autism Insurance Reform.* Accessed September 30, 2013, at http://www.autismspeaks.org/advocacy/ advocacy-news/welcome-34-oregon-enacts-autism-insurance-reform.

Bearss, K., Johnson, C., Smith, T., Lecavalier, L., Swiezy, N., Aman, M., . . . Scahill, L. (2015). Effect of parent training vs. parent education on behavioral problems in children with autism spectrum disorder: a randomized clinical trial. *JAMA, 313*, 1524-1533.

Bibby, B., Eikeseth, E., Martin, N.T., Mudford, O.C., & Reeves, D. (2001). Progress and outcomes for children with autism receiving parent managed intensive interventions. *Research in Developmental Disabilities, 22*, 245-447.

Bondy A., & Frost L. (1998). The Picture Exchange Communication System. *Seminars in Speech and Language, 19*, 373–389.

Boyd, B., Hume., K., McBee, M., Alessandri, M., Gutierrez, A., Johnson, L., et al. (2014). Comparative efficacy of LEAP, TEACCH and non-model-specific special education programs for preschoolers with autism spectrum disorders. *Journal of Autism and Developmental Disorders, 44,* 1-15.

Cohen, H., Amerine-Dickens, M., & Smith, T. (2006). Early intensive behavioral treatment: Replication of the UCLA Model in a community setting. *Journal of Developmental and Behavioral Pediatrics, 27*, S145-S155.

Dawson, G., & Burner, K. (2011). Behavioral interventions in children and adolescents with autism spectrum disorder: A review of recent findings. *Neurology, 23*, 616-620.

Dawson, G., Rogers, S., Munson, J., Smith, M., Winter, J., Greenson, J., … Varley, J. (2010). Randomized, controlled trial of an intervention for toddlers with autism: The Early Start Denver Model. *Pediatrics, 125*, 17-23.

Eikeseth, S., Hayward, D., Gale, C., Gitlesen, J., & Eldevik, S. (2009). Intensity of supervision and outcome for preschool aged children receiving early and intensive behavioral interventions: A preliminary study. *Research in Autism Spectrum Disorders, 3*, 67-73.

Eikeseth, S., Klintwall, L., Jahr, E., & Karlsson, P. (2012). Outcome for children with autism receiving early and intensive behavioral intervention in mainstream preschool and kindergarten settings. *Research in Autism Spectrum Disorders, 6*, 829–835.

Eikeseth, S., Smith, T., Jahr, E., & Eldevik, S. (2002). Intensive behavioral treatment at school for 4- to 7-year-old children with autism: A 1-year comparison controlled study. *Behavior Modification, 26*, 49–68.

Eikeseth, S., Smith, T., Eldevik, S., & Jahr, E. (2007). Outcome for children with autism who began intensive behavioral treatment between age four and seven: A comparison controlled study. *Behavior Modification, 31*, 264–278.

Eldevik, S., Eikeseth S., Jahr E., & Smith T. (2006). Effects of low-intensity behavioral treatment for children with autism and mental retardation. *Journal of Autism and Developmental Disorders, 36*, 211-224.

Eldevik, S., Hastings, R. P., Hughes, J. C., Jahr, E., Eikeseth, S. & Cross, S. (2009) Meta-analysis of early intensive behavioral intervention for children with autism. *Clinical and Adolescent Psychology, 38*, 439-450.

Eldevik, S., Hastings, R. P., Hughes, J. C., Jahr, E., Eikeseth, S., & Cross, S. (2010). Using participant data to extend the evidence base for intensive behavioral intervention for children with autism. *American Journal on Intellectual and Developmental Disabilities, 115,* 381-405.

Flores, M., Musgrove, K., Renner, S., Hinton, V., Strozier, S., Franklin, S., & Hil, D. (2012). A comparison of communication using the Apple iPad and a picture-based system. *Augmentative and Alternative Communication, 28,* 74-84.

Frost, L., & Bondy, A. (2002). *A Picture's Worth: PECS and Other Visual Communication Strategies in Autism. Topics in Autism.* Bethesda, MD: Woodbine House.

Frost, L., & Bondy, A. (2003). Communication strategies for visual learners. In O. I. Lovaas (Ed.), *Teaching individuals with developmental delays: Basic intervention techniques* (pp. 271-306). Austin, TX: Pro-Ed.

Goods, K., Ishijima, E., Chang, Y., & Kasari, C. (2013). Preschool based JASPER intervention in minimally verbal children with autism: Pilot RCT. *Journal of Autism and Developmental Disorders, 43*, 1050-1056.

Granpeesheh, D., Dixon, D. R., Tarbox, J., Kaplan, A. M., & Wilke, A. E. (2009). The effects of age and treatment intensity on behavioral intervention outcomes for children with autism spectrum disorders. *Research in Autism Spectrum Disorders, 3*, 1014-1022.

Handleman, J. S. & Harris, S. L. (2001). *Preschool education programs for children with autism* (2nd ed.). Austin, TX: Pro-Ed.

Howard, J. S., Sparkman, C. R., Cohen, H. G., Green, G., & Stanislaw, H. (2005). A comparison of intensive behavior analytic and eclectic treatments for young children with autism. *Research in Developmental Disabilities, 26*, 359–383.

Interagency Autism Coordinating Committee (IACC). (2012). *IACC Strategic Plan for Autism Spectrum Disorder (ASD) Research—2012 Update.* Retrieved from the U.S. Department of Health and Human Services Interagency Autism Coordinating Committee website: http://iacc.hhs.gov/strategic-plan/2012/index.shtml.

Jacobson, J. W., Mulick, J. A., & Green, G. (1998). Cost-benefit estimates for early intensive behavioral intervention for young children with autism: General model and single state case. *Behavioral Interventions, 13,* 201–226.

Kaiser, A. P., & Hester, P. P. (1994). Generalized effects of enhanced milieu teaching. *Journal of Speech & Hearing Research, 37,* 1320-1340.

Kaiser, A. P., Yoder, P. J., & Keetz, A. (1992). Evaluating milieu teaching. In Warren, S. F. & Reichle, J. E. (Eds.) *Causes and effects in communication and language intervention* (pp. 9-47). Baltimore, MD, England: Paul H. Brookes Publishing.

Kasari, C. (2002). Assessing change in early intervention programs for children with autism. *Journal of Autism and Developmental Disorders, 32,* 447-462.

Kasari, C., Freeman, F., & Paparella, T. (2006). Joint attention and symbolic play in young children with autism: A randomized controlled intervention study. *Journal of Child Psychology and Psychiatry, 47,* 611-620.

Kasari, C., Gulsrud, A., Freeman, S., Paparella, T., & Hellemann, G. (2012). Longitudinal follow-up of children with autism receiving targeted interventions on joint attention and play. *Journal of the American Academy of Child & Adolescent Psychiatry, 51,* 487-495.

Kasari, C., Kaiser, A., Goods, K., Nietfeld, J., Mathy, P., Landa, R., . . . Almirall, D. (2014). Communication interventions for minimally verbal children with autism: A sequential multiple assignment randomized trial. *Journal of the American Academy of Child and Adolescent Psychiatry, 53,* 635-646.

Kasari, C., Paparella, T., Freeman, S., & Jahromi, L.B. (2008). Language outcome in autism: Randomized comparison of joint attention and play interventions. *Journal of Consulting and Clinical Psychology, 76,* 125-137.

Kasari, C., & Smith, T. (2013). Interventions in schools for children with autism spectrum disorder: Methods and recommendations. *Autism, 17,* 254-267.

Kasari, C., Smith, T., Lord, C., & Kaiser, A. (n.d.). *Adaptive interventions for minimally verbal children with ASD in the community (AIM-ASD).* In: ClinicalTrials.gov [Internet]. Bethesda (MD): National Library of Medicine (US). 2000- [cited 2013 Dec 16]. Available from: http://clinicaltrials.gov/ct2/show/study/NCT01751698. NLM Identifier: NCT01751698.

Kasari, C., Smith, T., & Landa, R. (n.d.). *Intervention for communication in autism network.* In: ClinicalTrials.gov [Internet]. Bethesda (MD): National Library of

Medicine (US). 2000- [17 Dec 2013]. Available from: http://clinicaltrials.gov/ct2/show/NCT01018407. NLM Identifier: NCT01018407.

Klintwall, L., & Eikeseth, S. (2011). Number and controllability of reinforcers and predictors of individual outcome for children with autism receiving early and intensive behavioral intervention: A preliminary study. *Research in Autism Spectrum Disorders, 6*, 493-499.

Layton, T., Yoder, P. (1988). Speech following sign language training in autistic children with minimal verbal language. *Journal of Autism and Developmental Disorders, 18*, 217-229.

Lovaas, O. I., Ackerman, A.B., Alexander, D., Firestone, P., Perkins, J., & Young, D. (1981). *Teaching developmentally disabled children: The ME book.* Austin, TX: Pro-Ed.

Lovaas, O. I. (1987). Behavioral treatment and normal educational and intellectual functioning in young autistic children. *Journal of Consulting and Clinical Psychology, 55,* 3–9

Lovaas, O. I., & Smith, T. (2003). Early and intensive behavioral intervention in autism. In A. E. Kazdin & J. R. Weisz (Eds.), *Evidence-based psychotherapies for children and adolescents* (pp. 325–340). New York, NY: Guilford Press.

Magiati, I., Charman, T., & Howlin, P. (2007). A two-year prospective follow-up study of community-based early intensive behavioural intervention and specialist nursery provision for children with autism spectrum disorders. *Journal of Child Psychology and Psychiatry, 48*, 803–812.

Maglione, M. A., Gans, D., Das, L., Timbie, J., & Kasari, C. (2012). Nonmedical interventions for children with ASD: Recommended guidelines and further research needs. *Pediatrics, 130,* S169-S178.

Mandell, D. S., Stahmer, A. C., Shin, S., Xie, M., Reisinger, E., & Marcus, S. C. (2013). The role of treatment fidelity on outcomes during a randomized field trial of an autism intervention. *Autism, 17*, 281-295.

McEachin, J. J., Smith, T., & Lovaas, O. I. (1993). Long-term outcome of children with autism who received early intensive behavioral treatment. *American Journal on Mental Retardation, 97*, 359–372.

Myers, S. M., & Johnson, C. P. (2007). Management of children with autism spectrum disorders. *Pediatrics, 120,* 1162-1182.

Oono, I. P., Honey, E. J., & McConachie, H. (2013). Parent-mediated early intervention for young children with autism spectrum disorders (ASD *Cochrane Database of Systematic Reviews, Issue 4.* Art. No.: CD009774. DOI: 10.1002/14651858.CD009774.pub2

Parsons, S., Charman, T., Faulkner, R., Ragan, J., Wallace, S., & Wittemeyer, K. (2013). Commentary--Bridging the research and practice gap in autism: the importance of creating research partnerships with schools. *Autism, 17*, 268-280.

Prizant, B. M., & Wetherby, A. M. (2005) Critical issues in enhancing communication abilities for persons with autism spectrum disorders. In Volkmar, F. R., Paul, R., Klin, A., & Cohen, D. (Eds.), *Handbook of autism and pervasive developmental disorders, Volume 2: Assessment, interventions, and policy* (3rd ed., pp. 925-945). Hoboken, NJ: Wiley.

Proloquo2Go. (2013). *Special purpose application: Assistive-Ware.* Accessed at http://www.proloquo2go.com/.

Reichow, B. (2012). Overview of meta-analyses on early intensive behavioral intervention for young children with autism spectrum disorders. *Journal of Autism and Developmental Disorders, 42*, 512-520.

Reichow B., Barton E. E., Boyd B. A., & Hume K. (2012). Early intensive behavioral intervention (EIBI) for young children with autism spectrum disorders. *Cochrane Database of Systematic Reviews,* Issue 10. Art. No.: CD009260.

Reichow, B., & Wolery, M. (2009). Comprehensive synthesis of early intensive behavioral interventions for young children with autism based on the UCLA Young Autism Project Model. *Journal of Autism and Developmental Disabilities, 39*, 23-41.

Remington, B., Hastings, R. P., Kovshoff, H., degli Espinosa, F., Jahr, W., Brown, T., . . . Ward, N. (2007). A field effectiveness study of early intensive behavioral intervention: Outcomes for children with autism and their parents after two years. *American Journal on Mental Retardation, 112*, 418–438.

Rogers, S. J. (n.d.). Intensive intervention for toddlers with autism. In: ClinicalTrials. gov [Internet]. Bethesda (MD): National Library of Medicine (US). 2000- [16 Dec 2013]. Available from: http://clinicaltrials.gov/ct2/show/NCT00698997. NLM Identifier: NCT00698997.

Sallows, G. D., & Graupner, T. D. (2005). Intensive behavioral treatment for children with autism: Four-year outcomes and predictors. *American Journal on Mental Retardation, 110*, 417–438.

Shane, H., Laubscher, E. H., Schlosser, R. W., Flynn, S., Sorce, J. F., & Abramson, J. (2012). Applying technology to visually support language and communication in individuals with autism spectrum disorders. *Journal of Autism and Developmental Disorders, 42*, 1228-1235.

Sheinkopf, S., & Siegel, B (1998). Home-based behavioral treatment of young children with autism. *Journal of Autism and Developmental Disorders, 28*, 15-23.

Sherer, M. R., & Schreibman, L. (2005). Individual behavioral profiles and predictors of treatment effectiveness for children with autism. *Journal of Consulting and Clinical Psychology, 73*, 525-538.

Simpson, R. L., Mundschenk, N. A., & Heflin, L. J. (2011). Issues, policies, and recommendations for improving the education of learners with autism spectrum disorders. *Journal of Disability Policy Studies, 22*, 3-17.

Smith, T., Groen, A. D., & Wynn, J. W. (2000). Randomized trial of intensive early intervention for children with pervasive developmental disorder. *American Journal on Mental Retardation, 4*, 269–285.

Smith, T. (2010). Early and intensive behavioral intervention in autism. In A. E. Kazdin and J. Weisz (Eds.), *Evidence-based psychotherapies for children and adolescents* (2nd ed., pp. 312-326). New York: Guilford Press.

Smith, T. (2011). *Making inclusion work for students with autism spectrum disorders: An evidence-based guide.* New York, NY: Guilford Press.

Smith, T., Klorman, R., & Mruzek, D. W. (2015). Predicting outcome of community-based early intensive behavioral intervention for children with autism. *Journal of Abnormal Child Psychology 43*, 1271-1282. doi: 10.1007/s10802-015-0002-2.

Strain, P. S., & Bovey, E. H. (2011). Randomized, controlled trial of the LEAP model of early intervention for young children with autism spectrum disorders. *Topics in Early Childhood Special Education, 3*, 133-154.

Strauss, K., Vicari, S., Valeri, G., D'Elia, L., Arima, S., & Fava, L. (2012). Parent inclusion in Early Intensive Behavioral Intervention: the influence of parental stress, parent treatment fidelity and parent-mediated generalization of behavior targets on child outcomes. *Research in Developmental Disabilities, 33*, 688-703.

Zarembo, A. (2011, December 11). Autism boom: An epidemic of disease or of discovery? *Los Angeles Times*. Retrieved from http://www.latimes.com/news/local/autism/la-me-autism-day-one-html,0,1218038.htmlstory.

A Review of Agency Websites Offering ABA Services in the Midwestern United States

Kimberly A. Zoder-Martell, Shannon Titus Dieringer, Allison C. Labrie, Caitlin M. Pistor, Neelima Duncan, and Jamie B. Gaither

Abstract

There has been an increase in the number of agencies offering early intervention services rooted in applied behavior analysis (ABA) to children with autism spectrum disorder (ASD) over the past several decades. Parents and caregivers need to be able to make informed decisions regarding treatment options for their children. Oftentimes, parents evaluate treatment options based on the information contained on agency websites, which is especially common when travel to multiple facilities is not feasible. In addition to helping parents make informed treatment decisions, it is important to ensure that these providers meet minimum quality standards given the proliferation of agencies that provide ABA services. Unfortunately, there is little empirical guidance regarding quality indicators for the provision of ABA services. The primary purpose of the current study is to explore content regarding ABA services reported on provider websites as this information is readily available to parents who may need to select services for their child. A secondary goal of this study was to compare the services described by ABA providers on their website to available quality indicators. These goals were accomplished by reviewing and coding 175 websites for ABA providers in the Midwestern United States. Descriptive data are presented and suggestions for additional quality indicators are included.

Keywords: applied behavior analysis, autism spectrum disorder, early intervention

Based on the most recent surveillance data from the Centers for Disease Control and Prevention (2012), the prevalence of 8-year-olds diagnosed with autism spectrum disorder (ASD) has increased to 1 in 68. Additionally, children are being identified at a younger age, with reliable diagnoses being rendered as early as infancy (Koegel, Koegel, Ashbaugh, & Bradshaw, 2014). Outcomes are generally thought to be more favorable when children with ASD are identified at an early age because early intervention services can be initiated before the developmental gap between children with ASD and their typically developing peers becomes more pronounced (Handleman & Harris, 2000; Wetherby & Woods, 2006). There is a substantial body of literature that demonstrates the effectiveness of early intervention services for improving outcomes for children with ASD (e.g., Lovaas, 1987; Wetherby & Woods, 2006) and the implementation of high quality interventions from an early age may reduce the lifetime cost of care for individuals with ASD by up to 65% (Ganz, 2007)

When a child is diagnosed with ASD, parents and caregivers must choose from amongst numerous treatment options and many wish to prioritize treatments that are demonstrated to be effective. This can be a daunting task for parents who often rely on professional recommendations, autism-related media, and websites to make treatment decisions (Miller, Schreck, Mulick, & Butter, 2012). The Internet, which is easily accessible to most parents, is often where parents begin researching interventions and local service providers. However, conflicting information found on the Internet may make it even more challenging for parents to differentiate between effective and ineffective services (Green, 2007; Smith & Antolovich, 2000). It is also important that professionals (e.g., psychologists, pediatricians, teachers), who are involved with the family at the forefront of a diagnosis, are able to assist parents with navigating information on the Internet regarding treatment options, and provide parents with guidance in selecting appropriate services based on available quality indicators and best practice.

Quality Indicators of ABA Services

There is a robust literature supporting the use of interventions rooted in ABA for increasing adaptive skills and decreasing problem behaviors in children with ASD (Foxx, 1996; Matson, Hattier, & Belva, 2012; National Autism Center, 2015). Over the last decade, there has been rapid growth in the number of agencies that provide ABA services to children with ASD and there may be variability in the quality of services offered by each provider. Unfortunately, there are no scientifically tested guidelines families can use when selecting ABA providers. However, advocacy and educational organizations have produced suggestions regarding quality indicators to assist parents in assessing services (e.g., Autism Speaks, 2012; Handleman & Harris, 2000; Los Angeles Area Families for Effective Autism Treatment [LAFEAT], n.d.; New Jersey Department of Education [NJDOE], 2004; New York Department of Education [NYDOE], 2001).

Without quality control measures in place, ABA providers are more likely to deviate from highly ethical and principled practice. In addition, the risk of abuse, which is already high among clients with limited communication skills (Wilczynski, Connolly, DuBard, Henderson, & McIntosh, 2015), is potentially heightened without clearly defined quality control measures. Additionally, preliminary research suggests that programs of questionable quality are associated with less improvement (Howard, Stanislaw, Green, Sparkman, & Cohen, 2014; Perry, Prichard, & Penn, 2006). Therefore, ensuring that programs meet minimum quality standards and employ effective and evidence-based strategies rooted in ABA is essential. If early intervention ABA services are deemed most appropriate for a child, professionals should be prepared to guide parents through the process of selecting an ABA provider using the available quality indicators.

Based on available recommendations, four themes have emerged with regard to quality indicators for ABA programs. Specifically, program intensity, the use of behavioral principles, a comprehensive curriculum, and staff qualifications are often sug-gested as key quality indicators for ABA programs (Gould, Dixon, Najdowski, Smith, & Tarbox, 2011; Hayward, Gale, & Eikeseth, 2009). It is imperative that professionals make parents aware of available ABA program quality indicators so they can make informed deci-sions when selecting early intervention providers given what is at stake for their child.

Program Intensity

The intensity of the intervention is an important consideration when selecting ABA programs for students with ASD. Intensity for comprehensive early behavioral intervention programs is defined in the literature as 30-40 hours per week (Gould et al., 2011; Lovaas 1987, Perry et al., 2006). Ideally, early intervention services should be provided for at least 30 hours per week for a minimum of two years (Eldevik, Eikeseth, Jahr, & Smith, 2006; Lovaas, 1987); however, there has been some evidence to suggest that fewer hours per week (i.e., 25 hours) may also be effective (Perry et al., 2008).

The literature on program intensity has focused primarily on young children with ASD (Howard et al., 2014; National Research Council, 2001). Early intervention (i.e., intervention prior to the age of 5) is directly linked to more favorable outcomes for children with ASD (Lovaas, 1987; Wetherby & Woods, 2006). When services are implemented at an earlier age, the child has the opportunity to receive intensive interventions for a longer period of time and during a critical phase of development.

Program intensity should be carefully considered based on the individualized needs of the child. Focused interventions designed to address behavior reduction or skill development will likely require a lower intensity. Parents seeking ABA services for their young children with ASD may not be aware of this distinction, therefore professionals should educate parents regarding the importance of individualizing program intensity. If comprehensive gains are needed across a wide array of skill domains (e.g., communication, social interaction, play, adaptive skills), higher intensity will be needed to produce meaningful gains.

Comprehensive Curriculum

The inclusion of a comprehensive curriculum based on the principles of ABA is also an important quality indicator. Although most of the available research cited the importance of carefully selecting program components, no specific guidelines for the selection of assessments or curricula are offered. A comprehensive program should minimally include a multi-modal and multi-informant assessment, individualization of program targets, and a uniform and consistent method of targeting skills, collecting data, and monitoring progress (Gould et al., 2011; Handleman & Harris, 2000; Perry et al., 2006). Additionally, the inclusion of family training may be ideal to promote the maintenance and generalization of skills across multiple environments (Gould et al., 2011; Matson, Mahan, & Matson, 2009). Other important components include a plan for transitioning to a less restrictive environment or school setting and access to peers (Handleman & Harris, 2000; NJDOE, 2004; NYDOE, 2001).

With regard to a comprehensive assessment, it is important to note that there is not one assessment that can reliably assess all areas of need for a child with ASD (Gould et al., 2011). Assessment procedures must be carefully considered, as these procedures will initially drive the development of an individualized intervention program. Program individualization is acknowledged as a core component of comprehensive ABA programming and should be incorporated when developing a quality curriculum (Handelman & Harris, 2000).

Quality of Staff and Supervision

ABA providers must employ qualified staff and supervisors (Autism Speaks, 2012; Gould et al., 2011; Hayward et al., 2009). Qualified staff is generally defined as professionals with advanced degrees, certifications, and experience in areas relating to education, behavior analysis, and autism (Gould et al., 2001). The Behavior Analysis Certification Board (BACB) offers several certifications including the Board Certified Assistant Behavior Analyst (BCaBA), Board Certified Behavior Analyst (BCBA), and Board Certified Behavior Analyst-Doctoral (BCBA-D), which ensure that clinicians meet minimal educational and supervision requirements prior to providing ABA services. Although not acknowledged by the BACB, the term "master clinician" is used by some in the field to identify those with the BCBA-D credential and at least 10 years of relevant experience (Shook, 2005). Certification through the BACB is not the only way to ensure competency to work with children who have ASD. For example, behavioral psychologists, school psychologists, and special education teachers who have specific training in ABA may also competently work with children with ASD.

In ABA centers, direct care staff often serve as the frontline therapists who are responsible for delivering early intervention services. It is highly recommended that direct care staff working with children who have ASD should be trained and supervised by qualified professionals to increase their capacity to address challenging behaviors and improve the skill repertoires of children served (Autism Speaks, 2012; NJDOE, 2004; NYDOE, 2001). In addition, providers are encouraged to consider client to staff ratio. Given the needs of children with ASD, it is recommended that centers maintain a low client to staff ratio where children can receive highly individualized intensive intervention and direct care staff is able to implement high quality services.

Purpose

Parents frequently consult websites when making decisions about selecting ABA providers for their child with ASD and they need to be positioned to make informed decisions based on the information presented by each provider. The primary purpose of this study was to evaluate the content that ABA providers in the

Midwestern United States (i.e., Illinois, Indiana, Michigan Ohio, Wisconsin) present on their websites to better understand the information available to families making treatment decisions for young children with ASD. The services described by ABA providers were then compared to the established quality indicators. The results serve as a foundation for recommendations for both ABA providers and families pursuing ABA intervention services.

Method

Identifying ABA Providers

ABA providers in the Midwest who have organizational websites were selected for inclusion in this study. There are several reasons why providers in the Midwest were prioritized for this study. It would be impossible to review all websites for multiple regions of the country because new ABA providers regularly establish agencies and an accurate assessment could not be completed. The Midwest was selected because it is likely that there are fewer provider options available than in many other regions and parents are more likely to face challenges in identifying an ABA provider. For example, there are an extremely large number of ABA providers available on each coast. Florida, in particular, has a large number of providers, perhaps because it was in this state that certification of behavior analysts was initiated. Parents in this region have many options from which to choose. By reviewing websites for ABA providers in the Midwest, we hope to highlight the importance of including information on ABA provider websites that is critical to families who are most likely to be challenged when attempting to find the right treatment fit for their child.

To identify organizations that provide ABA services to individuals with ASD in the Midwest, three graduate students conducted an Internet search using the websites Google (www.google.com), Autism Speaks (www.autismspeaks.org), the Autism Society of Illinois (www.autismillinois.org), and Maximum Potential Kids

Directory (www.maximumpotentialkids.com). The search terms "ABA center+ name of state" and "aba programming + name of state" were utilized when searching for and identifying organizational websites. These websites and search terms were used because they generate comprehensive lists of providers by state. Websites for agencies that did not provide ABA services to children with ASD were excluded. Of the 175 websites identified, 59 were found for the state of Illinois, 39 for Indiana, 21 for Michigan, 29 for Ohio, and 27 for Wisconsin.

Coding Strategy

The information on each website was coded for the presence or absence of variables related to key quality indicators for ABA programs (i.e., intensity, use of behavioral principles, staff qualifications, comprehensive programming; see Table 1). Each website was also rated on a three-point scale for ease of use (i.e., usability). Websites obtained a score of two when it was easy to find all the information on the coding sheet; a one when it was easy to find most information; and a zero when it was difficult to navigate the website. Websites were further coded based on whether the comprehensive information related to the variables of interest were available and earned a score of two when information was obtained for over 51% of the items on the coding sheet; a one if the website included information for 26% to 50% of variables on the coding sheet; and a zero if information for less than 25% of variables was included on the coding sheet.

Two independent observers coded 20% (n = 34) of the websites to establish interobserver agreement (IOA). IOA was calculated only for ease of navigating the website. Of all of the variables coded, ease of use was judged to be the most important variable if the goal is for parents to be able to evaluate ABA providers based on information included on the agency's website. Percent agreement was 82%.

Table 1:
Coding System

	Coding Methods
Intensity of Services	Recorded range of therapy hours per week, typical duration of therapy, age range of clients accepted.
Behavior Principles	Coded based on whether the providers offered services based on the behavioral principles of learning and motivation.
Comprehensive Programming	
Assessment	Assessment procedures reported by each provider were recorded. Items coded in this category included language and curriculum guides (e.g., VB-MAPP), academic achievement (e.g., Bracken), adaptive behavior (e.g., Vineland), developmental assessments (e.g., Bailey), diagnostic evaluation (e.g., ADOS-2), executive functioning (e.g. BRIEF), cognitive assessment (e.g., WISC-IV), social skills assessment (e.g., Social Skills Rating System), and functional behavior assessment.
Related Services	Related services presented on the website, including speech therapy, physical therapy, occupational therapy, psychiatry, case management, and social work were recorded.
Treatment Modalities	Coded for the presence of individual therapy, social skills groups, family therapy, family support groups, family training, discrete trial training, natural environment training, transitions services, school-based consultation service, medical consultation services or a combination of services offered.
Settings	Coded based on the setting in which services were delivered including home, school, center-based, outpatient, inpatient, tele-therapy/remote access therapy, or a combination of settings
Staff Characteristics	Staff characteristics included the presence of staff biographies, level of education, licenses and certifications (RBT, BCaBA, BCBA, BCBA-D), number of master clinicians on staff, and the number of licensed psychologists on staff.

Results

Program Intensity

A majority of the ABA provider websites did not describe program intensity (i.e., identify a recommended number of therapy hours per week). Specifically, only 23% of the center websites provided a minimum number of therapy hours required for treatment at their center. Of the providers that included this information, 80% offered a minimum number of hours less than what has been shown to be effective for comprehensive programming in the scientific literature (i.e., 25-40 hours per week). In fact, 100% of agencies in Illinois, 89% of agencies in Michigan, 85% of agencies in Indiana, 75% of agencies in Ohio, and 45% of agencies in Wisconsin offered fewer than 25 hours of therapy per week.

The websites were also analyzed to determine the age ranges of individuals who were eligible for therapy (Table 2). Most of the websites (84%) reported the age ranges of clients served. Of the providers who reported treatment age, 71% provide early intervention, 94% school-age treatment, and 43% provide services to adults.

Table 2:
Ages Served

	Midwest	Indiana	Ohio	Michigan	Illinois	Wisconsin
Early Intervention	71%	68%	70%	81%	69%	68%
School-Age	94%	91%	85%	95%	98%	100%
Adult	43%	38%	48%	29%	52%	41%

Note: These numbers represent the percentage based on the number of autism centers that reported on the ages of clients served.

Comprehensive Curriculum

Each website was reviewed for information on the type of assessment procedures employed (Table 3). Of the websites reviewed, only 26% reported the assessment procedures that were employed. The two most common assessments described were the Assessment of Basic Language and Learning Skills-Revised (ABLLS-R) and the Verbal Behavior Milestones Assessment and Placement Program (VB-MAPP). Additionally, 13% of ABA providers used the Autism Diagnostic Observation Schedule-2nd Ed (ADOS-2), and 11% reported using the Assessment of Functional Living Skills (AFLS).

Across providers, 12 treatment targets were identified (see Table 4). A majority (i.e., 82%) of websites in the Midwest cited specific skills that were targeted for improvement. The most commonly indicated treatment targets included social skills (91%), communication (84%), play and leisure skills (70%), life skills (65%), and academic skills (63%). Each website was also reviewed to determine if individualized treatment and family training were part of the comprehensive curriculum package (see Table 5). An overwhelming majority (77%) of ABA provider websites reported individualizing treatments and 64% offered family training.

Table 3:
Assessment Procedures

	Midwest	Indiana	Ohio	Michigan	Illinois	Wisconsin
VB-MAPP	71%	89%	17%	88%	86%	33%
ABLLS	42%	33%	17%	50%	57%	67%
ADOS	13%	0%	17%	13%	0%	67%
AFFLS	11%	11%	0%	13%	29%	0%

Note: These numbers represent the percentage of autism centers that reported staff qualifications.

Table 4:
Treatment Options

	Midwest	Indiana	Ohio	Michigan	Illinois	Wisconsin
Play/ Leisure Skills	70%	71%	65%	53%	82%	62%
Feeding/ Eating Skills	40%	37%	31%	40%	61%	14%
Toilet Training	40%	37%	38%	47%	54%	19%
Communication	84%	87%	92%	67%	85%	76%
Cooperation	41%	37%	27%	13%	83%	5%
Social	91%	84%	96%	87%	98%	86%
Life Skills	65%	68%	62%	67%	80%	33%
Fine Motor Skills	40%	26%	58%	27%	51%	29%
Academic Skills	63%	55%	88%	47%	76%	33%
Compliance	11%	13%	8%	7%	7%	19%
Functional Communication Training (FCT)	20%	13%	42%	13%	10%	29%
Self-Injurious Behavior (SIB)	14%	18%	31%	7%	10%	0%

Note: These numbers represent the percentage of autism centers that reported types of treatments utilized.

Qualified Staff and Supervision

Nearly two-thirds of the websites (65%) described staff qualifications (see Table 6) with 94% of providers reporting at least one employee with a Master's degree. The number of employees with Master's degrees varied significantly based on the provider (i.e., 1-56), presumably depending on the size and number of clients

Table 5:
Comprehensive Treatment

	Midwest	Indiana	Ohio	Michigan	Illinois	Wisconsin
Individualized Treatment	77%	87%	83%	76%	70%	75%
Family Training	64%	62%	69%	81%	48%	88%

Note: These numbers represent the percentage based on the number of autism centers that reported individualized treatment and family training.

served by the organization. Over half (i.e., 51%) of the ABA providers across the Midwest reported employing at least one individual with a doctoral degree (range, 1-20 per organization). Only 19% of centers in the Midwest reported having staff members with a BCaBA, while a much larger percentage (i.e., 72%) had at least one BCBA on staff (range, 1-31). Of the centers that reported employee qualifications, only 16% employed a BCBA-D, and only 5% suggested staff meeting the qualifications for a master clinician. In addition, 31% of autism centers employed at least one psychologist, which is noteworthy because some insurance companies require oversight by a psychologist.

Ease of website use and comprehensive information

The mean ease of use score across all websites was .84 (range 0 to 2). The mean comprehensive information score for each state is as follows: Indiana (1.10), Michigan (1.15), Ohio (.67), Illinois (.53), and Wisconsin (1.0). Overall, the websites were difficult to navigate and did not often contain comprehensive information regarding available services.

Discussion

The prevalence of children diagnosed with ASD is increasing and there is a growing need for comprehensive and effective

Table 6:
Staff Qualifications for ABA Providers in the Midwest

	Midwest	Indiana	Ohio	Michigan	Illinois	Wisconsin
Masters level staff	94%	100%	94%	94%	87%	89%
Doctoral Degree	51%	46%	56%	35%	47%	84%
BCaBA	19%	36%	33%	9%	7%	11%
BCBA	72%	93%	67%	82%	67%	32%
BCBA-D	16%	14%	39%	3%	13%	21%
Master Clinicians	5%	7%	11%	0%	0%	11%
Psychologists	31%	32%	28%	15%	20%	68%

Note: These numbers represent the percentage of autism centers that reported staff qualifications.

interventions. Interventions rooted in the principles of ABA are ideal for addressing the needs of children with ASD and are supported in the literature (NAC, 2015). Furthermore, when intervention services can be initiated during early childhood, outcomes are generally thought to be more favorable (Handleman & Harris, 2000; Wetherby & Woods, 2006). Oftentimes, children are diagnosed with ASD prior to the age of 8 and parents generally seek out services as soon as a diagnosis is provided. When evaluating services, parents often begin their search with a review of websites (Miller et al., 2012). ABA agencies are at liberty to decide what information to include on their websites. In some cases, interventions that are not supported in the literature (e.g., hyperbaric treatment) may also be promoted. Families affected by ASD deserve easy access to information that can help them select the right treatment for their children. Families must be well-positioned to quickly identify an appropriate provider based on quality indicators for comprehensive programs and their child's specific needs. Professionals involved with the family should also be equipped to provide parents with guidance in selecting ABA providers.

The primary purpose of this study was to review the websites of ABA providers in the Midwest and compare the services discussed on the website to quality indicators for ABA programs recommended by advocacy and educational organizations. A commonly recommended guideline states that young children with ASD benefit from early intensive behavioral services. When reviewing data regarding the intensity of services described on ABA provider websites, a majority of these agencies did not indicate the number of hours clients were expected to complete each week. Most ABA provider websites in the Midwest indicated that fewer than 25 hours of therapy per week was an option. The exception to this outcome is Wisconsin, where less than half of ABA providers reported offering services for less than 25 hours per week. This difference may have emerged because the Wisconsin Early Autism Project (WEAP) is a large-scale project that has served as a replication site for Lovaas's (1987) groundbreaking work. Researchers associated with WEAP have published significant research on comprehensive early intervention for children with ASD. As a result, programs in Wisconsin may be more likely to report a large number of hours are needed to match the needs of most young children with ASD. In contrast, ABA providers that are not a replication site may not emphasize the importance of this quality indicator. This may particularly be the case in states in which insurance companies regularly reject requests for more intensive services. In addition, it may be encouraging that some ABA agencies agree to provide services for fewer than 25 hours when young children with ASD can meet the goals of treatment with less intense intervention. That is, some parents may seek the services of a behavior analyst not for comprehensive services for their child but instead, for a focused purpose (e.g., toileting, self-injury, sleep disturbance). Families may also not seek comprehensive services due to resource constraints. Intensity of services may need to be individualized based on the unique needs and situation of each young child. However, ABA providers must take care to ensure families are aware that the likelihood of producing extensive changes across relevant skill and behavioral domains (e.g., communication, play, social and adaptive skills, etc.) is negligible when comprehensive services are not provided to children with extensive needs.

The issue of intensity may interact meaningfully with the age of the child at time of initial service delivery. When young children begin receiving services at an earlier age they have the opportunity for a longer and more intensive course of therapy. The best available evidence shows that early intensive behavioral intervention for the treatment of ASD is most effective. Typically, early intervention refers to services obtained prior to the age of 5 (Gould et al, 2011; Jacobson, Mulick, & Green, 1998; Love, Carr, Almason, & Petursdottir, 2009; Smith, Klorman, & Mruzek, 2015), although services prior to the age of 8 are sometimes considered "early intervention." It is promising that 71% (range 68% to 81%) of the ABA providers serve children during early childhood because access to comprehensive treatment during this developmental period is associated with the greatest outcomes. However, the vast majority of ABA providers indicated they offered services to school-aged children (range 85% to 100%) and this may be a reason so many ABA providers do not identify a minimum number of therapeutic hours per week on their websites. Older children may be in school during the day and require only supplemental services. Although the current study focuses on information gleaned from websites involving young children with ASD, it is noteworthy that some individuals may require therapy services through adulthood. Research regarding effective interventions for adults with ASD is much more limited compared to the available research targeting children (NAC, 2015). It is encouraging that 43% of centers provide services to adults with ASD since this is traditionally an under-served population.

When comprehensive programming is needed (e.g., during the early childhood period), most providers reported relying on the VB-MAPP and ABLLS-R for treatment planning. Although a majority of ABA providers delivered intervention services related to areas of known deficits for children with ASD (i.e., communication skills, social skills, academic skills), a paucity of information about assessment tools used to plan the treatment trajectory were identified on the websites. Few ABA providers described their use of other interventions that may benefit clients with ASD (e.g., compliance training, academic skills, and functional communication training). Despite the fact that children with ASD often engage in higher rates of self-injurious behavior (SIB) than other children, few ABA providers reported addressing the needs of children with SIB.

Family training is also an important component to help provide parents with the skills to meet the needs of their child with ASD. In Wisconsin, 88% of ABA providers stated they delivered parent training, whereas only 48% of centers in Illinois reported family training. Having a child with a disability is known to increase parental stress (Neely-Barnes & Dia, 2008). Therefore, it is important to equip parents with the skills necessary to meet the needs of their child. In addition, delivering parent training during the early childhood years can benefit behavioral and learning outcomes during elementary school (McIntyre, 2008).

With regard to staff qualifications, a majority of ABA providers employ clinicians with a BCBA. This qualification requires the clinician to have completed a Master's Degree in ABA or other related field (e.g., education, psychology) and have obtained supervised hours in the provision of behavior analysis. Fewer agencies reported to employ BCaBAs and doctoral level staff including BCBA-Ds and psychologists. The BCBA is the most commonly awarded credential from the BACB with far fewer certificants holding the BCaBA or BCBA-D (http://bacb.com/about-the-bacb/). An even smaller percentage of centers indicated having a "master clinician" on staff. Interestingly, this credential is not recognized by the BACB, but is sometimes discussed in the scientific literature and in professional settings (e.g., Shook, 2005).

This study was exploratory in nature with the goal of identifying services offered by ABA providers in the Midwest, and comparing information that is readily available on a provider's website to quality indicators. The methodology involved reviewing all services solely based on information contained on each agency's website. It is certain that some agencies provide services that were not clearly specified on the organizational website. To obtain a fuller understanding of the services ABA agencies provide, future investigators should directly measure the services that are offered.

One of the goals of this study was to assess the extent to which providers employ qualified staff. Although information regarding staff qualifications and credentials were available on many websites, degrees and credentials do not necessarily ensure competency or quality services. An important component that should be further explored is client to staff ratios. Based on information provided on agency websites it is impossible to assess this potentially important variable because the number of clients served by each provider is not reported on the websites. This is a variable that parents should inquire about when contacting ABA providers. Therapist to client ratios is an important quality indicator and should be evaluated in future studies.

Another limitation of this study is related to individuals who recently earned the Registered Behavior Technician (RBT) credential. The RBT is an entry-level credential for individuals practicing ABA that ensures minimum training standards are met. In recent months, this credential has become more common; however, at the time of data collection, this credential was less common. It is potentially important to have data regarding the number of RBTs that a provider employs because additional supervisors would be required.

Despite the limitations, this study still has potential implications for the provision of ABA services. When locating an ABA provider, it is conceivable that parents will first complete an Internet search. Provider websites should include current and comprehensive information so that the audience viewing their site (e.g., parents, potential clients) has a clear understanding of what they are offering. Second, this study draws attention to the lack of available quality indicators for ABA programs. As they continue to proliferate, it is important to develop clear quality indicators to evaluate ABA programs. This is especially prudent given that the "quality" of treatment may be directly linked to child outcomes.

Although it is obvious that intensity, the use of behavioral interventions, comprehensive programming, and employing qualified staff are certainly important, there are additional factors that should be considered when selecting ABA providers. For one, it is important to evaluate financial information (e.g., self-pay, insurance accepted, sliding fees) in order to have a better understanding of out of pocket costs. Additionally, there is some information that may be useful in making treatment decisions that cannot be gleaned from reviewing a website (e.g., client to staff ratio). Parents should be made aware of these factors to ask relevant questions.

Another consideration is community involvement. Although this is not unanimously identified as a quality indicator, it demonstrates the provider's investment in the larger community and allows for outreach and support. Providers could increase community involvement through newsletters, blogs, community presentations, links to additional community resources, and/or through social media. These practices are common in other early childhood settings and help to foster a sense of community and collaboration. Additionally, community involvement helps raise awareness of ASD and local services beneficial for the ASD population.

Finally, although a number of ABA providers report meeting minimum quality standards, it is apparent that a number also offer services that are not supported in the literature and may be in conflict with the underlying tenets of ABA (e.g., sensory integration therapy, hyperbaric treatment). Although this was not the goal of the current study, professionals should understand these practices and should encourage families to seek early intervention services supported in the literature.

Author's Note:

Address correspondence to Kimberly A. Zoder-Martell, Ph.D., HSPP, BCBA-D; Ball State University; 2000 W. University Ave, TC 711, Muncie, IN, 47303; kamartell@bsu.edu. The authors would like to acknowledge Daniel Kamer and Madeline Daly for their assistance with data collection.

References

Autism Speaks (2012). Applied behavior analysis: A parent's guide. Retrieved from https://www.autismspeaks.org/science/resources-programs/autism-treatment-network/atn-air-p-applied-behavior-analysis

Centers for Disease Control and Prevention. (2012). Morbidity and mortality weekly report: Prevalence of autism spectrum disorders – Autism and developmental disabilities monitoring. *Surveillance Summaries, 61*(3), 1-19.

Eldevik, S., Eikeseth, S., Jahr, E., & Smith, T. (2006). Effects of low-intensive behavioral treatment for children with autism and mental retardation. *Journal of Autism and Developmental Disorders, 36*(2), 211–224.

Foxx, R. M. (1996). Twenty years of applied behavior analysis in treating the most severe problem behavior: Lessons learned. *Behavior Analyst, 19*(2), 225-235.

Ganz, M. L. (2007). The lifetime distribution of the incremental societal costs of autism. *Archives of pediatrics & adolescent medicine, 161*(4), 343-349.

Gould, E., Dixon, D. R., Najdowski, A. C., Smith, M. N., & Tarbox, J. (2011). A review of assessments for determining the content of early intensive behavioral intervention programs for autism spectrum disorders. *Research in Autism Spectrum Disorders, 5*(3), 990-1002.

Green, V.A. (2007). Parental experience with treatments for autism. *Journal of Developmental and Physical Disabilities, 19*(2), 91-101.

Handleman, J. S., & Harris, S., (Eds.). (2000). *Preschool Education Programs for Children with Autism* (2nd Ed). Austin, TX: Pro-Ed.

Hayward, D. W., Gale, C. M., & Eikeseth, S. (2009). Intensive behavioural intervention for young children with autism: A research-based service model. *Research in Autism Spectrum Disorders, 3*(3), 571–580.

Howard, J. S., Stanislaw, H., Green, G., Sparkman, C. R., & Cohen, H. G. (2014). Comparison of behavior analytic and eclectic early interventions for young children with autism after three years. *Research in Developmental Disabilities, 35*(12), 3326-3344. doi:10.1016/j.ridd.2014.08.021

Jacobson, J. W., Mulick, J. A., & Green, G. (1998). Cost-benefit estimates for early intensive behavioral intervention for young children with autism - General model and single state case. *Behavioral Interventions, 13*, 201-226.

Koegel, L. K., Koegel, R. L., Ashbaugh, K., & Bradshaw, J. (2014). The importance of early identification and intervention for children with or at risk for autism spectrum disorders. *International Journal of Speech-Language Pathology, 16*(1), 50-56. doi:10.3109/17549507.2013.861511

Los Angeles Area Families for Effective Autism Treatment (LAFEAT) (n.d.). Components of a quality ABA program. Retrieved from http://www.lafeat.org/web/aba_components/

Lovaas, O. I. (1987). Behavioral treatment and normal educational and intellectual functioning in young autistic children. *Journal of Consulting and Clinical Psychology, 55*(1), 3–9.

Love, J. R., Carr, J. E., Almason, S. M., & Petursdottir, A. I. (2009). Early and intensive behavioral intervention for autism: A survey of clinical practices. *Research in Autism Spectrum Disorders, 3*, 421-428.

Matson, J. L., Hattier, M. A., Belva, B. (2012). Treating adaptive living skills of persons with autism using applied behavior analysis: A review. *Research in Autism Spectrum Disorders, 6*(1), 271-276.

Matson, M. L., Mahan, S., J. L. & Matson, J. L. (2009). Parent training: A review of methods for children with autism spectrum disorders. *Research in Autism Spectrum Disorders, 3*(4), 868–875.

McIntyre, L. L. (2008). Parent training for young children with developmental disabilities: Randomized controlled trial. *American Journal of Mental Retardation, 113*(5), 356-368.

Miller, V. A., Schreck, K. A., Mulick, J. A., & Butter, E. (2012). Factors related to parents' choices of treatments for their children with autism spectrum disorders. *Research in Autism Spectrum Disorders, 6* (1), 87-95.

National Autism Center. (2015). *National Standards Report: Phase2*. Retrieved from http://www.nationalautismcenter.org/pdf/NAC%20Standards%20Report.pdf.

National Research Council. (2001). *Educating children with autism: Committee on educational interventions for children with autism*. Washington, D.C.: National Academy.

Neely-Barnes, S. L. & Dia, D. A. (2008). Families of children with disabilities: A review of literature and recommendations for interventions. *Journal of Early and Intensive Behavior Intervention, 5*(3), 93-107.

New Jersey Department of Education. (2004). *A self-review and quality improvement guide for programs serving young students with autism spectrum disorders*. Retrieved from http://www.nj.gov/education/specialed/info/autism.pdf

New York Department of Education. (2001). *A self-review and quality improvement guide for schools and programs serving students with autism*. Retrieved from http://files. eric.ed.gov/fulltext/ED458767.pdf

Perry, A., Cummings, A., Dunn Geier, J., Freedman, N. L, Hughes, S., LaRose, L., ...& Williams, J. (2008). Effectiveness of intensive behavioral intervention in a large community-based program. *Research in Autism Spectrum Disorders, 2*(4), 621-642.

Perry, A., Prichard, E. A., & Penn, H. E. (2006). Indicators of quality teaching in intensive behavioral intervention: A survey of parents and professionals. *Behavioral Interventions, 21*(2), 85-96. doi:10.1002/bin.212

Shook, G. L. (2005). An examination of the integrity and future of the Behavior Analyst Certification Board® credentials. *Behavior Modification, 29*(3), 562-574.

Smith, T., & Antolovich, M. (2000). Parental perceptions of supplemental interventions received by young children with autism in intensive behavior analytic treatment. *Behavior Interventions, 15*(2), 83-97.

Smith, T., Klorman, R., & Mruzek, D.W. (2015). Predicting outcome of community based early intensive behavioral intervention for children with autism. *Journal of Abnormal Child Psychology, 43*(7). 1271-1282.

Wetherby, A., & Woods, J. (2006) Early social interaction project for children with autism spectrum disorders beginning in the second year of life: A preliminary study. *Topics in Early Childhood Special Education, 26*(2), 67-82.

Wilczynski, S. M., Connolly, S., Dubard, M., Henderson, A., & Mcintosh, D. (2015). Assessment, prevention, and intervention for abuse among individuals with disabilities. *Psychology in the Schools, 52*(1), 9-21.

Gross Motor Needs for Children With Autism Spectrum Disorder to Enhance the Educational Experience

Shannon Titus Dieringer, Kimberly A. Zoder-Martell, and Caitlin M. Pistor

Abstract

The Diagnostic and Statistical Manual of Mental Disorders (5th ed.), lists the common characteristics associated with autism spectrum disorder (ASD) to include deficits in social and communication skills; and the presence of restricted, repetitive patterns of behavior, interests, and activities (American Psychiatric Association, 2013). However, children with ASD often exhibit deficits in other areas as well, including gross motor skills (GMS). GMS are large physical body movements used to move from one place to another (e.g., walking) or manipulate large objects (e.g., throwing). GMS are most commonly associated with sport-related activities and are often overlooked when developing programming in the early intervention setting. When developing programs in the early intervention setting it is of particular importance to consider programming for GMS because research suggests GMS, social skills, and academic skills are closely intertwined (Pagani & Messier, 2012). The purpose of this paper is to review briefly GMS deficits commonly observed in children with ASD and to discuss further the potential relationship between social and academic skills. Then current practices of programs delivered in the early intervention setting will be examined. Finally, general suggestions for educators and caregivers of children with ASD interested in developing and incorporating GMS programming into existing early intervention programs will be reviewed.

Key words: gross motor, autism, early intervention

In the United States, early intervention services for children with autism spectrum disorder (ASD) are increasingly prevalent (Reichow, Barton, Boyd, & Hume, 2014). It is not uncommon to see center-based programs in a community that utilize several evidence-based practices to address the common deficits of children with ASD including, but not limited to, social, communication, and behavior skills (American Psychiatric Association, 2013).

Early intervention programs often include ongoing, intensive care, educational services, and interventions for young children with disabilities (including those with ASD) or those children suspected to be at risk for developmental delays before entering kindergarten (National Research Council, 2001). The impact of early intervention programs for students with ASD has been well-documented in the literature (Fernell et al., 2011; Lovaas, 1987; Remington et al., 2007; Smith, Groen, & Wynn, 2000). The majority of early intervention utilize research-based programs and are very successful at promoting academic, communication, functional life, play, social and intellectual functioning skills (Fernell et al., 2011; Lloyd, MacDonald, & Lord, 2013; Lovaas, 1987; Remington et al., 2007; Smith et al., 2000). Perhaps the most common evidence-based practice utilized in early intervention settings is applied behavior analysis (ABA) (Lovaas, 1987; Weiss and Delmolino, 2006). More specifically, evidence-based practices utilize instructional strategies that allow for multiple opportunities to respond (OTR) and are matched with the student's specific skill deficit(s), in his or her natural setting (Bellini & Peters, 2007). Early intervention programs that have utilized this approach have demonstrated increases in social and communication skills and improvement in adaptive behaviors.

There is a wealth of research supporting the use of early intervention services for children with ASD. Unfortunately, often these programs focus on the core deficits observed in students with ASD and neglect programming for the unique gross motor needs evident in children with ASD.

Gross Motor Needs of Children with ASD

In addition to the core symptoms of ASD, children with ASD often present with gross motor skills (GMS) deficits. GMS are body movements that involve large muscles (e.g., arms, legs, whole body) and are responsible for moving and manipulating oneself and other objects (Esposito & Vivanti, 2013). Common gross motor limitations observed in children with ASD include bradykinesia (i.e., slowness of movement); apraxia/dyspraxia (i.e., difficulty with motor planning and sequencing of movements); abnormalities of gait and posture (e.g., toe-walking, rigidity); and akinesia/dyskinesia (i.e., difficulty initiating or switching movements, freezing or stopping movement, as well as deficits in muscle tone (i.e., hypotonia) and general gross motor delays (American Psychiatric Association, 2013; Ming, Brimacombe, & Wagner, 2007).

The acquisition of typical gross motor behaviors (i.e., sitting, crawling, walking) has been found to mature at a slower rate and reach full maturity at later times in children with ASD than their typically developing peers (Ozonoff et al., 2008). These GMS deficits often present soon after birth (Berkeley, Zittel, Pitney, & Nichols, 2001; Provost, Lopez, & Heimerl, 2007) and can impact children's adaptive functioning across multiple domains, including the development of social skills. Furthermore, the development of early social skills and emotional understanding may influence academic readiness skills by allowing children to form meaningful relationships with their teachers and peers, as well as engage and attend more to classroom instruction (Elias & Haynes, 2008; Izard et al., 2001; Rhoades, Warren, Domitrovicha, & Greenberg, 2011).

Although there is a voluminous amount of research regarding GMS instructional strategies and interventions (e.g., Goodway & Branta, 2003), little research has been conducted to evaluate interventions specifically designed to meet the needs of young children with ASD. Furthermore, although there is some emerging research related to GMS interventions in the early intervention setting, a gap exists between the literature and what is practiced. The purpose of this paper is to provide parents, teachers, and early interventionists with an overview of the GMS needs of children with ASD. Also, the current gross motor assessment and intervention practices relevant to early intervention settings will be discussed. Finally, recommendations for specific programming and best teaching practices to promote GMS acquisition and physical activity levels in children with ASD will be offered. Children with ASD often engage in disruptive and off-task behaviors in physical activity settings (Lavay, Leary, & Hill, 1966).

The disruptive and off-task behaviors of children with ASD can be potentially explained by examining the known deficits in GMS and physical activity levels and the prevalence of noncompliance among children of ASD to teacher-directed tasks (Berkeley et al., 2001; Staples & Reid, 2010). Berkeley, Zittel, Pitney, and Nichols, (2001) and Staples and Reid (2010) conducted studies to examine the fundamental motor skills (FMS) (object control and locomotor skills) levels of young children with ASD using the Test of Gross Motor Development -2 (TGMD-2). Berkeley et al., (2001) concluded 73% of all children were in the poor to very poor categories for both locomotor and object control skills when compared to their age-matched peers without their disabilities. Additionally, Staples and Reid (2010) utilized groups of 25 participants diagnosed with ASD and compared them to three other groups: 1) chronological age matched group; 2) developmentally matched group; and 3) mental age matched group. The researchers concluded that the participants diagnosed with ASD were more delayed in their FMS when compared to any other group in the study.

Additionally, Provost, Lopez, and Heimerl, (2007) compared the motor delays of young children with ASD, developmental delays, and developmental concerns. The study included 56 children ranging from 21 to 41 months diagnosed with ASD (*n* = 19), developmental delays and motor delays (*n* = 19), or developmental delays with no motor delays (*n* = 18). It was concluded participants with ASD had significant delays in GMS when compared to their same-aged peers with developmental delays/concern for developmental delays.

When the results of these studies are combined and synthesized, it is evident that children with ASD present with GMS deficits that should be addressed through early intervention. Furthermore, these studies open the potential for dialog concerning other skills that may be impacted by GMS limitation in children with ASD.

Research on Motor Skills Interventions

Although early intervention programs have been very successful at addressing and supporting many deficits common in children with ASD, areas of known deficits (i.e., GMS) are often left unaddressed. Occupational therapy is a standard intervention for children with motor skills deficits and can be used to improve areas such as FMS, coordination, and play skills; however, few interventions that focus on these areas of functioning have been validated by research (Dawson & Watling, 2000). Furthermore, some studies have examined the direct assessment and effectiveness of a structured intervention to improve GMS in this setting; however, research is beginning to emerge that focuses on effective GMS interventions for children with ASD in the early intervention setting. Available literature has focused on motor skills (MS; i.e., GMS, fine motor skills, motor coordination, motor planning, and adaptive motor skills) in social and educational settings throughout childhood and adolescence (Berkley et al., 2001; Ghaziuddin & Butler, 1998; MacDonald, Lord, & Ulrich, 2013b; Stoit, van Schie, Slaats-Willemse, & Buitelaar, 2013).

Intervention and instructional strategies to promote functional, fine, and GMS, such as visual, verbal, and physical supports (Breslin & Rudisill, 2011; Reid, Collier, & Cauchon, 1991); structured motor skills practice (Duronjić, & Válková, 2010; Finn & Válková, 2007); and MS practice through social skills training (Gutman et al., 2010; Lloyd et al., 2013) have all been effective at promoting MS development for children and adolescents with ASD. What is lacking from the literature, however, is the use of these strategies in early intervention settings to specifically target GMS that is essential for social and academic functioning. By understanding what strategies have been successful in promoting motor skills in youth with ASD, the authors hope to use this information to present potential instructional strategies that may be modified and incorporated in the early intervention setting for children with ASD.

As documented in the literature, there has been much research on the use of visual supports and their effectiveness in improving GMS of students with ASD. Reid, Collier, and Cauchon (1991) investigated the effects of using visual, verbal, and physical prompting on the acquisition of a GMS (e.g., rolling a bowling ball) for four children between the ages of 11 and 15 who were diagnosed with ASD and compared verbal prompts and visual prompts with verbal prompts and physical prompts. At the conclusion of the intervention, it was determined that verbal/visual and the verbal/physical prompting models were both successful. More recently, Breslin and Rudisill (2011) investigated the use of visual supports to supplement instructions and demonstrations during a gross motor skills assessment (i.e., TGMD-2). The researchers found the use of picture cards in addition to auditory instructions elicited a higher gross motor score on TGMD-2 in children with ASD. Therefore, it can be concluded that additional prompting is essential at promoting GMS acquisitions.

As a whole, the motor/movement intervention literature suggests preschoolers with disabilities (e.g., ASD) benefit from structured, teacher-directed activity programs (Breslin & Rudisill, 2011; Duronjić, & Válková, 2010; Finn & Válková, 2007; Reid et al., 1991) and supports the need for GMS interventions. Specifically, Finn and Válková (2007) and Duronjić, and Válková (2010) conducted an individualized GMS intervention study and found individualized GMS interventions that occurred for 30 and 60 minutes, respectively, were effective in increasing GMS. The findings of these studies suggest that although time and resource intensive interventions are ideal, even interventions that are provided at a lower dose with fewer resources still result in positive GMS development.

Along with structured MS focused interventions, promoting participation in exercise and physical activity allows children with ASD to improve GMS, while encouraging healthy behaviors. Similar to others, children with ASD also benefit from a regularly scheduled, structured fitness program to promote the acquisition of MS and physical activity behaviors. Most successful physical activity interventions occur several days per week (e.g., 3 out of 5 school days) for 20 minutes to 1 hour (Lochbaum & Crews, 2003; Pan, 2011; Pitetti, Rendoff, Grover, & Beets, 2007; Srinivasan, Pescatello, & Bhat, 2014). The activities included in these programs incorporate GMS practice, muscular strength, aerobic endurance, and aquatic-focused activities. Early intervention GMS training can be helpful in developing these skills before formal schooling is started. Opportunities to participate in physical activity with peers is greater for younger students due to recess and physical education; however, these opportunities decrease as students age (Rosser Sandt & Frey, 2005). Therefore, it is essential that GMS deficits are addressed early to ensure children with ASD have adequate skills needed to engage in activity later in life.

Connection Between Skill Deficits and Academics

There may be a reciprocal relationship between social skill development and GMS (Berkley et al., 2001; Green et al., 2009; Staples & Reid, 2002). In children without disabilities, social skills often develop through developmental play (Pellegrini & Smith, 1998). Developmental play refers to the active physical interaction between two children and is essential for social growth, development of communication skills, and emotional regulation for all children, especially for individuals with ASD (Wolfberg, Bottema-Beutel, &

DeWitt, 2012). Skills such as cooperation, creativity, and helpful behaviors, often learned in early developmental play, are essential to appropriate classroom behavior (e.g., attention, motivation, and positive attitudes toward learning) (Coolahan, Fantuzzo, Mendez, & McDermott, 2000). Additionally, developmental play may allow for children to develop and practice their GMS (MacDonald et al., 2013; Pellegrini & Smith, 1998).

Although GMS deficits are not considered core diagnostic symptoms of ASD, these deficits can impact children with ASD by interfering with the acquisition of developmental play skills. Specifically, children with ASD may lack GMS to interact with peers in an age-appropriate manner, which may interfere with the developmental of social skills. However, because children with ASD often lack the social and communication skills to play successfully with their peers, they commonly miss opportunities to practice their GMS (MacDonald, Clark, Garrigan, & Vangala, 2005; MacDonald et al., 2013; Pan, 2008).

Appropriate social skills may also allow for the development of necessary classroom behavior and school readiness skills. Cooper and colleagues (2014) examined the relationship between kindergarten students' early social skills and their academic skills in fifth grade. The authors found high levels of appropriate social skills in early kindergarten predicted high academic performance levels in fifth grade. Furthermore, early prosocial skills have been found to be particularly predictive of later literacy skills (Miles & Stipek, 2006). Several studies have found social-emotional competence and knowledge can have positive effects on classroom behavior, which may lead to increased engagement in the classroom and an increased understanding related to the emotional and social cues of the teacher (Elias & Haynes, 2008; Izard et al., 2001; Rhoades et al., 2011). Although the relationship between social skills and academic readiness can be bidirectional (Caemmerer & Keith, 2014), social skills may also act as protective factors for students who have low academic skills in early childhood (Elias & Haynes, 2008).

In addition to the relationship between social skills and academic skills (AS), there is limited research suggesting GMS may have an impact on AS, especially during later childhood (Bornstein, Hahn, & Suwalsky, 2013; Son and Meisels, 2006). Specifically, GMS proficiency can be linked to academic achievement (Son & Meisels, 2006; Westendorp, Hartman, Houwe, Smoth, & Visscher, 2011). For example, Son and Meisels (2006) found early motor skills in kindergarten, especially visual motor skills, were related to first-grade cognitive achievement. Additionally, Westendorp et al., (2011) reported a positive correlation between locomotor skills and reading and a positive trend emerged between object control and mathematics. Although it is not clear whether AS impact GMS or vice versa, there seems to be a correlation between the two (Leary & Hill, 1996; Lloyd et al., 2013; Provost et al., 2007). Further investigation is warranted to develop a better understanding regarding the potential correlation between GMS and AS and to ensure we are meeting the needs of children with ASD.

The correlation between GMS, social skills, and academic achievement is becoming more apparent in the literature and should be considered in programming for children with ASD (Broun, 2009; Stichter, O'Connor, Herzog, Lierheimer, & McGhee, 2012). Because social skills, GMS, and AS in children with ASD are likely intertwined (White, Keonig, & Scahill, 2007) and can impact children's overall social, emotional, health, and academic success, it is important to address these variables together (Jasmin, Couture, McKinley, Reid, Fombonne, & Gisel, 2009). To date, early interventions have placed emphasis on improving the core deficits of children with ASD while promoting academic skills. Given the purported relationship between GMS, social skill deficits, and other developmental skill areas (e.g., academic skills), interventions to address GMS deficits in children with ASD should be developed and implemented (Gutman et al., 2010). We would like to propose a shift in practice to consider GMS development in children with ASD. Specifically, GMS activities should be incorporated into early intervention programs. In doing so, core deficits that are common in children diagnosed with ASD can continue to be addressed, while ensuring GMS deficits are also targeted. Ideally, GMS interventions should be implemented before children enter school to allow for extended practice and mastery of skills (Duronjić & Válková, 2010). By acquiring GMS at an early age (i.e., in the early intervention setting), children with ASD are more likely to participate in social situations that involve physical activity with their peers and more favorable academic outcomes may also be observed.

What Needs to be Included in Motor Skill Intervention Programs

Although gross motor programming is not commonly implemented in early intervention programs, beyond unstructured play (e.g., recess) or individually focused intervention (e,g., physical therapy, occupational therapy), research regarding GMS deficits in young children with ASD are becoming more prevalent in the literature. Specifically, successful interventions and instructional strategies have emerged that could be implemented in the early intervention setting. GMS interventions seen in the early intervention setting are commonly those conducted by occupational therapists and or adapted physical educators (Case-Smith, 1996). The goals of occupational therapy interventions in early education settings are to reduce the amount of motor impairment and increase participation in play and functional skills through individualized programs emphasizing developmental and learning principles (Case-Smith, Frolek Clark, & Schlabach, 2013). The purpose of adapted physical education (APE) is to provide individualized physical fitness, fundamental motor skills, and individual and group games and sport programming designed to meet the unique needs of children with disabilities (Winnick, 2011). Both individual and small group therapies have been shown to be effective in improving visual-motor skills in young children, as well as promoting kindergarten readiness and social skills (Case-Smith et al., 2013; Favazza et al., 2013). However, occupational therapists and adapted physical educators are not always present in early education settings. Therefore, it is important for early intervention educators to understand how to design and implement early motor skill development programs. When this is done successfully, improvements in motor skill acquisition and competence in young children can be seen (Robinson, Webster, Logan, Lucas, & Barber, 2012).

Instructional Strategies for Implementing Motor Skill Interventions

Although the research shows that there is a need, and a benefit, of GMS and physical activity interventions to improve overall motor, social, and academic skill success, interventions are not always readily apparent in practice. In a study which investigated the current services offered by early intervention programs (via website information), it was concluded that less than half of providers reported incorporating formal motor skills assessment or interventions into their curriculum (Zoder-Martell, Dieringer, Labrie, & Pistor, in review). Therefore, it is essential that we encourage such programming to promote the long-term success of children with ASD. Because social and motor skills are closely related it may be beneficial to incorporate activities that address deficits in all areas. Additionally, it is important to utilize research-based practices when developing interventions to help ensure their success (Williams-Taylor, 2007). The following section will address some key areas essential to successful implementation of motor skill programming for early intervention programs.

Gross motor skills. It is important to assess foundational GMS during early intervention programs to ensure children are building a solid skill foundation for future physical activity (Goodway & Branta, 2003). When choosing skills to include in your GMS programs, it is essential that both locomotor (i.e., movement skills) and object control (i.e., manipulation skills) are included. The TGMD-2 assessment used in the Breslin and Rudisill (2011) study is a norm-referenced

GMS assessment of six locomotor skills (e.g., running, skipping, galloping, leaping, jumping, and hopping) and six object control skills (e.g., throwing, catching, kicking, rolling, dribbling, and striking) (Ulrich, 2003). Programs should incorporate these twelve GMS skills to ensure children have a quality foundation of GMS.

Dosage. The Centers for Disease Control and Prevention (CDC; 2014b) recommends children should engage in at least 60 minutes of physical activity per day. The activities can be 60 minutes or more of moderate-to-vigorous aerobic, muscle-strengthening or bone-strengthening activity. Unfortunately, children with ASD are less likely to engage in these types of activities when compared to their peers due to delays in gross motor ability and coordination (Berkeley et al., 2001; Pan, 2008; Srinivasan et al., 2014; Staples & Reid, 2010). To promote the acquisition of positive motor skills and behaviors effectively, as well as increase muscular strength and endurance, individuals with ASD, like other populations, benefit from a regularly scheduled, structured fitness program. The most successful physical activity required participants to meet several times a week for sessions ranging from 20 minutes to 1 hour (Lochbaum & Crews, 2003; Pan, 2011; Pitetti et al., 2007; Srinivasan et al., 2014). Therefore, early intervention programs should include regular GMS based practice three or more days a week lasting at least 20 minutes to ensure positive skill development (Goodway & Branta, 2003).

Additional prompting. Individuals with ASD often have poor attention, especially when auditory information is presented (Gardner & Wolfe, 2013). Visual directions, as opposed to verbal directions, display abstract constructs of a task in a concrete way that is easier for many individuals with ASD to understand and process (Minshew, Meyer, & Goldstein, 2002). When developing motor skill programming, concepts such as running, jumping, and throwing can be abstract to a child with ASD (Breslin & Rudisill, 2011). Engaging in such tasks is often discouraged in other settings (e.g., being reprimanded for throwing an object at a peer); therefore, teaching the appropriate time to engage in a given motor task is essential. Teachers can develop social stories to encourage when, why, and where it is appropriate to engage in a motor task (e.g., It is fun to run in motor skills class.). Another helpful strategy to aid in keeping children with ASD on task during motor skill programming is visual schedules. By providing children with ASD a visual picture schedule, it will help with transitioning between tasks, attending to tasks for a prescribed time, and learning the actual GMS that is being taught. Finally, providing pictorial, verbal, and physical prompts during skill practice will allow children to understand the instructions given to them. For example, when practicing striking a ball off a baseball tee, a teacher can remind children to "squish the bug" with their foot to encourage trunk rotation and proper follow through of the strike. See Table 1 for examples of other potential verbal cues that are age and developmentally appropriate for children. It is important to note that verbal cues should be related to children's interest and can be changed accordingly based on the children. Additionally, taking a picture of an appropriate "striking" skill and posting it close to the activity will provide children with a visual example of the skill. When providing GMS instruction, it is important to provide different methods of instruction (e.g., prompts) for instructions to remain clear for children. Utilizing multiple prompting methods ensures that children have multiple opportunities to be exposed to and understand the tasks being presented.

Making learning fun. For many children with ASD, because they are "not good" at motor skills and physical activity, "they do not enjoy it" (Pan & Frey, 2006). Therefore, it is important to make skill practice fun, while encouraging multiple opportunities to respond (OTR) correctly. By increasing the OTR of specific skills, children are more likely to learn the skill (Goodway & Branta, 2003; Robinson et al., 2013). However, when asked to practice skills that are of low interest or are perceived as difficult to children, it is hard to keep them on task. One method of increasing the "fun" factor

Table 1:
Verbal Cues for Fundamental Motor Skill Success

Object Control Skills		Locomotor Skills	
Throw	*To remind child to step with opposition, place a sticker on the opposite foot of the throwing arm. State to the child…"Step with your sticker foot."*	Run	*To help remind the child to run smooth without pounding his/her feet, state to the child "fast feet like a cheetah."*
Catch	*To help the child the child catch the ball, toss a teddy bear or other stuffed animal and state the to child… "Give the bear a hug."*	Jump	*To remind the child to use their arms to get both feet of the ground and jump far (not bounce), state to the child… "Use those arms, jump like Ant-Man."*
Kick	*To create a better follow through after the kick the ball state to the child…"Kick as hard as you can."*	Skip	*After the child can hop (not before) the child can work on skipping. To help with the rhythm of the skip. State to the child… "Step, hop, step, hop, step, hop…"*
Roll	*To remind the child to roll the ball on the ground (not throw it), state to the child…."Don't let the egg crack."*	Gallop	*To help with the rhythm of the gallop and prevent tripping state to the child…"your front foot is in a race with your back foot, don't let your back foot catch your front foot."*
Dribble	*To remind the child not to "slap" the ball to the ground, state to the child "pretend your hand is like a spider going up its web."*	Leap	*To remind the child to take off from one foot and land on the other, state to the child…"Leap over the river."*
Striking	*To remind the child to rotate their hips during their swing and help with power and follow through without losing control of his/her body state to the child "Keep your foot on the ground and squish the bug with your foot."*	Hop	*Prior to starting hopping the child needs to be able to balance on one foot. Place objects on the floor (e.g., laminated leaf cut outs with tape on them) and have him/her pick them up with his/her feet. State to the child…"Pick up all the leaves that fell of the tree."*

of GMS practice and programming, is to provide a theme to the skill presented. For example, you can develop a theme around going to the beach (e.g., throwing and catching a beach ball, striking the coconuts out of the coconut tree). By incorporating a theme into the motor skill activities, children often forget they are learning and instead view each task as "playing."

Expanding beyond skill practice. Another perspective in encouraging physical activity and gross motor-focused activities is by teaching the concepts of games and activities. Often, skill practice becomes redundant and much like "work." One of the key issues of encouraging motor skill development and increased physical activity is that it is not fun, and it's hard. By creating an atmosphere which provides a safe environment to learn how to play a "game," children are more likely to want to try to play that game other places. For example, children with ASD often have difficulty understanding abstract ideas and concepts such as offense and defense, which is essential to playing almost any physical game. By providing opportunities for children to practice these concepts in a very structured manner (e.g., two-sided tag game), children can learn basic game concepts while practicing GMS (e.g., running). Programs can be created to encourage the development of motor and social skills through game play, and other peer interactions (e.g., talking to a teammate) can be used to promote these skills. GMS can be increased through play and peer interaction; mixed ability level groups can be used as models and can reinforce and motivate children with lower GMS (Case-Smith et.al., 2013). Research has found after teaching students with ASD different athletic group games, students showed greater participation in the games and mastery of the GMS required. The students also displayed greater amounts of speech and appropriate play (i.e., following the rules; Miltenberger & Charlop, 2014).

Summary

It is increasingly important that the characteristics and needs of children with ASD are understood. Furthermore, educators, parents, and caregivers must focus on early intervention which targets areas of deficit while still addressing their strengths. Currently, there is an emphasis on the importance of social competence and the early mastery of social skills to increase later academic success (Preston, 2015). However, this can be implemented throughout the early intervention curriculum by including motor skill programming. By focusing on GMS based programs, teachers can incorporate skills and concepts that they are already teaching into interactive and health focused activities. In doing so, children with ASD can improve essential skills identified as core deficits of their disability while improving other related areas of concern. Ensuring that early intervention programs incorporate motor skill programs into their curriculum is essential to the overall well-being of their students. By bringing awareness to the need of such programming and incorporating some of the suggestions from this paper, we hope to start a trend of encouraging motor skill practice and physical activity.

Author Note

Correspondence concerning this article should be addressed to Shannon Titus Dieringer, Department of Special Education, Ball State University, Muncie, IN 47304. Contact: sdieringer@bsu.edu

References

American Psychiatric Association. (2013). *Diagnostic and statistical manual of mental disorders* (5th ed.). Washington, DC: Author.

Bellini, S., & Peters, J. K. (2007). Social skills training for youth with autism spectrum disorders. *Child and Adolescent Psychiatric Clinics of North America, 17*(4), 857. doi:10.106/j.chc.2008.06.008

Berkeley, S. L., Zittel, L. L., Pitney, L. V., & Nichols, S. E. (2001). Locomotor and object control skills of children diagnosed with autism. *Adapted Physical Activity Quarterly, 18*(4), 405–416.

Bornstein, M. H., Hahn, C., & Suwalsky, J. D. (2013). Physically developed and exploratory young infants contribute to their own long-term academic achievement. *Psychological Science, 24*(10), 1906-1917.

Breslin, C. M., & Rudisill, M. E. (2011). The effect of visual supports on performance of the TGMD-2 for children with autism spectrum disorder. *Adapted Physical Activity Quarterly, 28*, 342-353.

Broun, L. (2009). Take the pencil out of the process. *Teaching Exceptional Children, 42*(1), 14-21.

Caemmerer, J. M., & Keith, T. Z. (2015). Longitudinal, reciprocal effects of social skills and achievement from kindergarten to eighth grade. *Journal of School Psychology, 53*(4), 265-281. doi:10.1016/j.jsp.2015.05.001

Case-Smith, J. (1996). Fine motor outcomes in children who receive occupational therapy services. *American Journal of Occupational Therapy, 50*, 52-61. doi:10.5014/ajot.50.1.52.

Case-Smith, J., Frolek Clark, G. J., & Schlabach, T. L. (2013). Systematic review of interventions used in occupational therapy to promote motor performance for children ages birth–5 years. *American Journal of Occupational Therapy, 67*, 413–424. doi:http://dx.doi.org/10.5014/ajot.2013.005959

Centers for Disease Control and Prevention (2014). *State Indicator Report on Physical Activity, 2014*. Department of Health and Human Services, Atlanta, GA: U.S.

Coolahan, K., Fantuzzo, J., Mendez, J., & McDermott, P. (2000). Preschool peer interactions and readiness to learn: Relationships between classroom peer play and learning behaviors and conduct. *Journal of Educational Psychology, 92*(3), 458-465. doi:10.1037/0022-0663.92.3.458

Cooper, B. R., Moore, J. E., Powers, C. J., Cleveland, M., & Greenberg, M. T., (2014) Patterns of early reading and social skills associated with academic success in elementary school. *Early Education and Development, 25*(8), 1248-1264. doi:10.1080/10409289.2014.932236

Dawson, G., & Watling, R. (2000). Interventions to facilitate auditory, visual, and motor integration in autism: A review of the evidence. *Journal of Autism and Developmental Disorders, 30*(5), 415-421.

Duronjić, M., & Válková, H. (2010). The influence of early intervention movement programs on motor skills development in preschoolers with autism spectrum disorders (Case Studies). *Acta Universitatis Palackianae Olomucensis. Gymnica, 40*(2), 37-45.

Elias, M. J., & Haynes, N. M. (2008). Social competence, social support, and academic achievement in minority, low-income, urban elementary school children. *School Psychology Quarterly, 23*(4), 474-495. doi:10.1037/1045-3830.23.4.474

Esposito, G., & Vivanti, G. (2013). Gross motor skills. In *Encyclopedia of Autism Spectrum Disorders* (pp. 1459-1462). New York: Springer.

Favazza, P. C., Siperstein, G. N., Zeisel, S. A., Odom, S. L., Sideris, J. H., & Moskowitz, A. L. (2013). Young athletes program: Impact on motor development. *Adapted Physical Activity Quarterly, 30*(3), 235-253.

Fernell, E., Hedvall, Å., Westerlund, J., Carlsson, L. H., Eriksson, M., Olsson, M. B., ... & Gillberg, C. (2011). Early intervention in 208 Swedish preschoolers with autism spectrum disorder. A prospective naturalistic study. *Research in Developmental Disabilities, 32*(6), 2092-2101.

Finn, K., & Válková, H. (2007). Motor skill development in preschool children with mental and developmental disorders: The difference after a one year comprehensive education program. *Acta Universitatis Palackianae Olomucensis. Gymnica, 37*(4), 91-98.

Gardner, S., & Wolfe, P. (2013). Use of video modeling and video prompting interventions for teaching daily living skills to individuals with autism spectrum disorders: A review. *Research and Practice for Persons with Severe Disabilities, 38*(2), 73-87.

Ghaziuddin, M., & Butler, E. (1998). Clumsiness in autism and Asperger syndrome: A further report. *Journal of Intellectual Disability Research, 42*(1), 43-48.

Goodway, J. D., & Branta, C. F. (2003). Influence of a motor skill intervention on fundamental motor skill development of disadvantaged preschool children. *Research Quarterly for Exercise and Sport, 74*(1), 36-46.

Green, D., Charman, T., Pickles, A., Chandler, S., Loucas, T., Simonoff, E., & Baird, G. (2009). Impairment in movement skills of children with autistic spectrum disorders. *Developmental Medicine and Child Neurology, 51*(4), 311–316. doi:10.1111/j.1469-8749.2008.03242.x

Gutman, S. A., Raphael, E. I., Ceder, L. M., Khan, A., Timp, K. M., & Salvant, S. (2010). The effect of a motor-based, social skills intervention for adolescents with high-functioning autism: two single-subject design cases. *Occupational Therapy International, 17*(4), 188-197. doi:10.1002/oti.300

Izard, C., Fine, S., Schultz, D., Mostow, A., Ackerman, B., & Youngstrom, E. (2001). Emotion knowledge as a predictor of social behavior and academic competence in children at risk. *Psychological Science (Wiley-Blackwell), 12*(1), 18-23.

Jasmin, E., Couture, M., McKinley, P., Reid, G., Fombonne, E., & Gisel, E. (2009). Sensori-motor and daily living skills of preschool children with autism spectrum disorders. *Journal of Autism & Developmental Disorders, 39*(2). 231-241 11p. doi:10.1007/s10803-008-0617-z

Lavay, B., Leary, M. R., & Hill, D. A. (1996). Moving on: Autism and movement disturbance. *Mental Retardation, 34*(1), 39-53.

Lloyd, M., MacDonald, M., & Lord, C. (2013). Motor skills of toddlers with autism spectrum disorders. *Autism: The International Journal of Research and Practice, 17*(2), 133-146.

Lochbaum, M., & Crews, D. (2003). Viability of cardiorespiratory and muscular strength programs for the adolescent with autism. *Complementary Health Practice Review, 8*(3). 225-233

Lovaas, O. I. (1987). Behavioral treatment and normal educational and intellectual functioning in young autistic children. *Journal of Consulting and Clinical Psychology, 55*(1), 3-9. doi:10.1037/0022-006X.55.1.3

MacDonald, R., Clark, M., Garrigan, E., & Vangala, M. (2005). Using video modeling to teach pretend play to children with autism. *Behavioral Interventions, 20*(4), 225-238. doi:10.1002/bin.197

MacDonald, M., Lord, C., & Ulrich, D. A. (2013). The relationship of motor skills and social communicative skills in school-aged children with autism spectrum disorder. *Adapted Physical Activity Quarterly, 30*, 271-282.

MacDonald, M., Lord, C., & Ulrich, D. (2013b). The relationship of motor skills and adaptive behavior skills in young children with autism spectrum disorders. *Research In Autism Spectrum Disorders, 7*(11), 1383-1390. doi:10.1016/j.rasd.2013.07.020

Milcs, S. B., & Stipek, D. (2006). Contemporaneous and longitudinal associations between social behavior and literacy achievement in a sample of low-income elementary school children. Child Development, 77(1), 103-117. doi:10.1111/j.1467-8624.2006.00859.x

Miltenberger, C., & Charlop, M. (2014). Increasing the athletic group play of children with autism. *Journal of Autism and Developmental Disorders, 44*(1), 41-54. doi:10.1007_s10803-013-1850-7

Ming, X., Brimacombe, M., & Wagner, G.C. (2007). Prevalence of motor impairment in autism spectrum disorders. *Brain and Development, 29*(9), 565-570.

Minshew, N. J., Meyer, J., & Goldstein, G. (2002). Abstract reasoning in autism: A dissociation between concept formation and concept identification. *Neuropsychology, 16*(3), 327-334.

National Research Council. (2001). *Educating children with autism*. Washington, D.C.: National Academy Press.

Ozonoff, S., Young, G. S., Goldring, S., Griess-Hess, L., Herrera, A. M., Steele, J., … Rogers, S. J. (2008). Gross motor development, movement abnormalities, and early identification of autism. *Journal of Autism and Developmental Disorders, 38*(4), 644-656. doi: :10.1007/s10803-007-0430-0.

Pagani, L. S., & Messier, S. (2012). Links between motor skills and indicators of school readiness at kindergarten entry in urban disadvantaged children. *Journal of Educational and Developmental Psychology 2*(1), 95-107.

Pan, C. Y., & Frey, G. C. (2006). Physical activity patterns in youth with autism spectrum disorders. *Journal of Autism and Developmental Disorders, 36*(5), 597-606. doi: 10.1007/s10803-006-0101-6

Pan, C. Y. (2008). Objectively measured physical activity between children with autism spectrum disorders and children without disabilities during inclusive recess settings in Taiwan. *Journal of Autism and Developmental Disorders, 38*(7), 1292-1301.

Pan, C. Y. (2011). The efficacy of an aquatic program on physical fitness and aquatic skills in children with and without autism spectrum disorders. *Research in Autism Spectrum Disorders, 5*(1), 657-665.

Pellegrini, A., & Smith, P. K. (1998). Physical activity play: The nature and function of a neglected aspect of play. *Child Development, 69*(3), 577.

Pitetti, K. H., Rendoff, A. D., Grover, T., & Beets, M. W. (2007). The efficacy of a 9-month treadmill walking program on the exercise capacity and weight reduction for adolescents with severe autism. *Journal of Autism and Developmental Disorders, 37*, 997-1006.

Preston, K. (2015). It's elementary: Social skills boost academics. *ASHA Leader, 20*(9), 48-54 7p.

Provost, B., Lopez, B. R., & Heimerl, S. (2007). A comparison of motor delays in young children: Autism spectrum disorder, developmental delay, and developmental concerns. *Journal of Autism and Developmental Disorders, 37*(2), 321-328.

Reichow, B., Barton, E. E., Boyd, B. A., Hume, K. (2014). Early intensive behavioral intervention (EIBI) for young children with autism spectrum disorders (ASD): A systematic review. Campbell Systematic Reviews 2014:9, *Campbell Collaboration.* doi: 10.4073/csr.2014.9

Reid, G., Collier, D., & Cauchon, M. (1991). Skill acquisition by children with autism: Influence of prompts. *Adapted Physical Activity Quarterly, 8*(4), 357-366.

Remington, B., Hastings, R. P., Kovshoff, H., degli Espinosa, F., Jahr, E., Brown, T., & … Ward, N. (2007). Early intensive behavioral intervention: Outcomes for children with autism and their parents after two years. *American Journal on*

Mental Retardation, 112(6), 418-438. doi:10.1352/0895-8017(2007)112[418:EIBI OF]2.0.CO;2

Rhoades, B. L., Warren, H. K., Domitrovich, C. E., & Greenberg, M. T. (2011). Examining the link between preschool social–emotional competence and first grade academic achievement: The role of attention skills. *Early Childhood Research Quarterly, 26*(2), 182-191. doi:10.1016/j.ecresq.2010.07.003

Robinson, L. E., Webster, E. K., Logan, S. W., Lucas, W. A., & Barber, L. T. (2012). Teaching practices that promote motor skills in early childhood settings. *Early Childhood Education Journal, 40*(2), 79-86.

Rosser Sandt, D. D., & Frey, G. C. (2005). Comparison of physical activity levels between children with and without autistic spectrum disorders. *Adapted Physical Activity Quarterly, 22*(2), 146-159.

Smith, T., Groen, A. D., & Wynn, J. W. (2000). Randomized trial of intensive early intervention for children with pervasive developmental disorder. *American Journal on Mental Retardation, 105*(4), 269-285.

Son, S. H., & Meisels, S. J. (2006). The relationships of young children's motor skills to later reading and math achievement. *Merrill-Palmer Quarterly, 52*, 755–778. doi:10.1353/mpq.2006.0033.

Srinivasan, S. M., Pescatello, L. S., & Bhat, A. N. (2014). Current perspectives on physical activity and exercise recommendations for children and adolescents with autism spectrum disorders. *Physical Therapy, 94*(6), 875-889.

Staples, K. L., & Reid, G. (2010). Fundamental movement skills and autism spectrum disorders. *Journal of Autism and Developmental Disorders, 40*(2), 209-217.

Stichter, J., O'Connor, K., Herzog, M., Lierheimer, K., & McGhee, S. (2012). Social competence intervention for elementary students with aspergers syndrome and high functioning autism. *Journal of Autism & Developmental Disorders, 42*(3), 354-366. doi:10.1007/s10803-011-1249-2

Stoit, A. B., van Schie, H. T., Slaats-Willemse, D. E., & Buitelaar, J. K. (2013). Grasping motor impairments in autism: not action planning but movement execution is deficient. *Journal of Autism and Developmental Disorders, 43*(12), 2793-2806.

Ulrich, D. A. (2000). *Test of gross motor development* (2nd ed.). Austin, TX: Pro-Ed.

Weiss, M. J., & Delmolino, L. (2006). The relationship between early learning rates and treatment outcome for children with autism receiving intensive home-based applied behavior analysis. *The Behavior Analyst Today, 7*(1), 96-110. doi:10.1037/h0100140

Westendorp, M., Hartman, E., Houwen, S., Smith, J., & Visscher, C. (2011). The relationship between gross motor skills and academic achievement in children with learning disabilities. *Research in Developmental Disabilities, 32*(6), 2773-2779. doi:10.1016/j.ridd.2011.05.032

White, S. W., Keonig, K., & Scahill, L. (2007). Social skills development in children with autism spectrum disorders: A review of the intervention research. *Journal of Autism & Developmental Disorders, 37*(10), 1858-1868. doi:10.1007/s10803-006-0320-x

Williams-Taylor, L. (2007). Research review - Evidence-based programs and practices: What does it all mean? *Children's Services Council of Palm Beach County.* Retrieved from http://www.evidencebasedassociates.com/reports/research_review.pdf.

Winnick, J. P. (2011). *Adapted Physical Education and Sport.* New York, NY: Human Kinetics.

Wolfberg, P., Bottema-Beutel, K., & DeWitt, M. (2012). Including children with autism in social and imaginary play with typical peers: Integrated play groups model. *American Journal of Play, 5*(1), 55-80.

Zoder-Martell, K. A., Dieringer, S. T., Labrie, A. C., & Pistor, C. M., (accepted for publication). A review of agency websites offering ABA services in the Midwest United States. *Perspectives on Early Childhood Psychology and Education.*

Integrating Evidence-Based Practice Into Early Childhood Alternative Settings With Children With ASD

Susan M. Wilczynski, Beth A. Trammell, Nicole Caugherty, Kassie Shellabarger, Constance E. McIntosh, and Amanda Kaake

Abstract

The number of empirically supported treatments for autism spectrum disorder (ASD) continues to grow. Although this increase in treatment options increases the likelihood young children with ASD will access effective interventions, the task of finding the most appropriate treatment becomes more daunting. This may be particularly the case in settings that supplement or supplant early childhood settings due to the unique cultural or contextual factors associated with these settings. This article explores the application of evidence-based practice (EBP), a decision-making model, to select effective treatments for young children with ASD who are served in two of these alternative childhood settings (i.e., Montessori schools and daycare centers). Practitioners and professionals administrating these alternative early childhood settings often worry about the "goodness-of-fit" between effective treatments and the setting. Challenges in adopting these treatments can result from differences in philosophical assumptions, resource constraints, and/or environmental supports. We provide illustrative examples that show how effective treatments can be selected in these alternate settings without violating the cultural and contextual concerns.

Keywords: early childhood, Montessori, daycare, evidence-based practice, autism, autism spectrum disorder

Evidence-based practice (EBP) is a decision-making model that can be used to identify the best treatment for each specific client. EBP requires the use of sound professional judgment to integrate the best available scientific evidence with client values, preferences, and context (Slocum, 2014). Comprehensive reviews like the National Standards Project 2.0 (NAC, 2015) or the Evidence-Based Practice for Children, Youth, and Young Adults with Autism Spectrum Disorder Report (Wong et al., 2014) have used systematic reviews to identify effective treatments for young children with autism spectrum disorder (ASD). The National Professional Development Center has developed numerous training modules covering EBP that include step-by-step practice guides, implementations checklists, and tip sheets for professionals (National Professional Development Center on ASD, 2014). Parents, teachers, psychologists, and allied health professionals can use these freely available resources, or other systematic reviews, to select from an array of effective treatments for toddlers, preschoolers, and all young children on the spectrum.

However, these systematic reviews have identified *many* effective treatments so practitioners will need to make decisions about which treatment is best for a given client. In addition, practitioners realize that the unique client and contextual factors for a given case often differs significantly from the participants and the settings in which research was conducted. Because the situation (i.e., client and context) is not identical, practitioners are always selecting treatments that do not perfectly match the scientific evidence. To make treatments truly effective on a case-by-case basis, practitioners need to incorporate client and contextual variables that are relevant to the intervention selection process and overall success of the treatment, which is effectively what the EBP decision-making process does.

The EBP decision-making process begins with a practical question (e.g. "How can I increase Jamie's play with peers during less structured time?" or "How can we reduce Sheila's stereotypic behaviors?"). This question leads to the identification of a target behavior and observable goal. The practitioner then identifies which empirically supported treatment (EST) is most appropriate to meet that goal. Simply asking this question immediately reduces the number of treatment options. That is, the practitioner looks for ESTs that match the behavior (and the function of behavior when appropriate). Knowledge about client and contextual variables should then be used to select the treatment that is most appropriate for a specific client. Practitioners select treatments based on factors such as the client's age, developmental level, and skill set, as well as the setting in which the intervention will be implemented.

There are few examples in the autism literature about how client and contextual variables can be applied to the EBP decision-making process when interventions are being implemented in settings outside traditional school systems. Although traditional school services are legally available to all young children with ASD, these services may be supplanted (e.g., Montessori schools) or supplemented (e.g., daycare) by other early childhood options. The purpose of this article is to provide examples of how these client and contextual variables can influence treatment selection in alternative early childhood settings. Specifically, we show how, in addition to scientific evidence supporting treatments, client and contextual variables can influence treatment selection in Montessori schools and daycare settings. We selected Montessori schools and daycare settings as our examples because they represent extremely divergent settings in which services are offered to young children with ASD. Montessori schools are based on the constructivist perspective, which is different than the applied behavior analytic philosophies that underlie most currently identified ESTs. By highlighting the procedural similarities used by practitioners of both philosophies, we seek to show how specific treatments could be integrated into programming in a way that does not significantly violate the principles of each. Daycare settings serve as a strong example because the rate of turnover, level of training for staff members, and the limited educational goals of daycare settings make it one of the most difficult early childhood settings to include components of ESTs for ASD. These illustrative examples are designed to help practitioners understand how ESTs can be used in alternate settings in a way that resolves philosophical differences, resource constraints, or limited environmental supports. However, we are not advocating that all young children with ASD served in Montessori school and daycare should receive the identified ESTs. Even minor deviations related to these factors could result in the selection of a different, more appropriate EST.

Montessori Method

Practical Question and Target Behavior

Jamie is a 3-year-old with pre-academic and adaptive skills commensurate with his peers. He has relatively strong social-communication skills, as evidenced by frequent and appropriate social initiations with his Montessori teachers. His interactions with classmates are infrequent and typically occur when he approaches peers to solicit help. How can Jamie's teachers increase appropriate play with peers during less structured parts of the day? Jamie's target goal is increasing initiation of peer play from once a week to 3 times a day. This might include asking a peer to play a game or play interactively with a peer.

Empirically Supported Treatment Choices

A large number of treatment options have been identified by systematic reviews of the ASD treatment literature for young children. Many of these treatments are identified by both the NSP 2.0 (NAC, 2015) and/or Wong et al. (2014) systematic reviews. The following were supported by both reviews: Behavioral interventions (prompting, reinforcement, response interruption/ redirection, time delay), naturalistic teaching strategies, modeling/video modeling, parent training, Pivotal Response Treatment (PRT), and scripting. In addition, the following were supported by one review for young children (under 5-6): Early Intensive Behavioral Interventions (EIBI; NAC only), functional communication training (FCT; Wong et al., only), language training (production; NAC only), peer training (Wong et al., only), social narrative, social skills training (Wong et al., only), visual supports (Wong et al., only).

This large list demonstrates that a treatment cannot be selected exclusively based on scientific evidence because there are too many options available. In addition, practitioners must decide how to resolve discrepancies across systematic reviews. Ideally, treatments appear on both lists (as well as other systematic reviews), however, due to methodological differences, discrepancies will emerge. When discrepancies across systematic reviews exist for a given behavior or age group, evidence-based (EB) practitioners can analyze the nature of research support for the treatment as applied to other age groups or for different target behaviors. For example, although many treatments appeared on only one list (e.g., Wong et al., 2014), they have all been deemed effective for other behaviors or age groups on the other list (e.g., NAC, 2015). Practitioners will have to use professional judgment to determine if the differences across the systematic reviews have direct implications for their clients (e.g., when the target behavior and the age group is very different, this would represent weaker evidence).

Client Variables

Due to his strong social-communication skills, the following interventions should be given a lower priority or eliminated: EIBI, FCT, and language training. EIBI is too comprehensive for his needs. FCT and language training do not match his practical question.

Contextual Variables

Montessori school philosophy and environmental structure. The Montessori Method involves creating a learning environment to accommodate each child's specific needs (McKenzie & Zascavage,

2012) and teacher-to-student interactions are multidirectional. Children are encouraged to work at their own pace and repeatedly manipulate materials as a way of mastering a concept. Classrooms are physically spread out, with objects strategically placed according to the needs of individual students (Ansari & Winsler, 2014). The student follows his or her own interest during many self-selected learning activities that are based on the child's developmental level. This is a discovery model in which the arrangement of the environment allows for engagement with a wide range of materials, help-seeking opportunities, and independence (Al, Sari, & Kahya, 2012). Because of the philosophical assumptions of the Montessori method, naturalistic strategies based on applied behavior analysis are likely to be a better fit to help Jamie. Of the remaining ESTs that increase play among young children with ASD, the following may be a good match with the philosophy and structure of Montessori schools: Behavioral interventions (when prompting and reinforce-ment in the form of encouragement are emphasized), naturalistic teaching strategies, modeling/video modeling, PRT, peer training, social narrative, social skills training, visual supports. Scripting is given a lower priority because it is not generative (i.e., it is highly prescriptive).

Other contextual variables. The EB practitioner then discusses the ESTs with Jamie's Montessori teachers. The following factors should be reviewed: cost of resources/materials required to imple-ment ESTs, the level of training needed, the level of adult direction required, and treatment acceptability (i.e., the extent to which his teachers find the treatment to be palatable, appropriate, and fair). In Jamie's case, the Montessori teachers reported that they already used scaffolding (which is procedural similar to prompting) and encouragement for success (which is procedurally similar to reinforcement), so they would be comfortable using these strate-gies. They were concerned about how frequently video modeling would have to be used because it could be distracting to other children. They found naturalistic teaching strategies (e.g., incidental teaching) and PRT to be very acceptable, but were concerned about the level of structure that might be required with PRT. The Montessori teachers did not care for the amount of adult direction that was necessary for peer training and believed their current approach to social skills training should be maintained. They believed social narrative (e.g., Social StoriesTM) and visual supports would be fine. When asked to rank-order their preferences, they identified naturalistic teaching strategies and video modeling (if used infrequently) as their top choices.

Integrating Client and Contextual Variables into Treatment

Naturalistic teaching strategies and video modeling were both selected because they are ESTs, match Jamie's specific needs closely, and were ranked as highly acceptable by Jamie's Montessori teachers. Incidental teaching is one naturalistic teaching strategy that is highly consistent with the Montessori Method and would involve a minimal degree of modification for use with Jamie. Incidental teaching occurs during situations that are naturally occurring and child-selected. Although incidental teaching was developed to improve language development (e.g., labeling and describing objects; Hart & Risley, 1968; 1975), it has also been used to increase social interactions (McGee, Almeida, Sulzer-Azaroff, & Feldman, 1992). The social partner builds on verbal and non-verbal cues from the child to encourage additional appropriate behavior (e.g., communication, social interactions). Like the Montessori Method, incidental teaching relies on the creation of a rich and varied environment that evokes behaviors associated with knowledge and skill acquisition. In this case, when Jamie initiates peer interaction, the teacher facilitates the development of new skills by prompting him and seeking elaborations on his initial efforts. For example, as Jamie steps closer to a peer who is playing, the teacher could give Jamie a verbal cue, such as "Hi, could I play trains with you?" Peer incidental teaching has resulted in increasing peer initiations and generalization of increased peer interactions in early childhood settings (McGee, et al., 1992).

By adopting incidental teaching for young children with ASD in a Montessori setting, the practical question (i.e., increasing peer interactions) can be improved without serious violations of the philosophical assumptions of the setting. Although incidental teaching is associated with a higher level of prompting, scaffolding is an acceptable strategy for Montessori teachers to use. Further, brief training in the use of incidental teaching has produced powerful outcomes (Ryan, Hemmes, Sturmey, Jacobs, & Grommet, 2008). Thus, the intrusiveness of having an outside specialist train staff in how to use incidental teaching in a Montessori setting would be minimal.

Video modeling involves the viewing of a video in which another person demonstrates the correct way to perform a given skill (Miltenberger & Charlop, 2015). Video modeling is an EST for young children with ASD (National Autism Center, 2015) and has been used to increase adaptive skills (e.g., toilet training; McLay, Carnett, van der Meer, & Lang, 2015), joint attention (Rudy, Betz, Malone, Henry, & Chong, 2014), and other appropriate social behaviors (Jones, Lerman, & Lechago, 2014) for young children. Despite the fact that advanced technology is not a mainstay of Montessori classroom, video modeling has the advantage of requiring minimal training for Montessori teachers. Videos could be developed by outside consultants (e.g., psychologists, behavior analysts) and could be shown to Jamie on portable devices in a secluded area so that the technological device does not intrude into the Montessori activity (e.g., circle time, free play, etc.). The Montessori school did not include creating the videos or playing them on a television in their budget. For this reason, Jamie's parents provided the videos and a portable device to Jamie's Montessori teachers.

Daycare Settings

Practical Question and Target Behavior

Sheila is a 2 ½ -year-old with ASD who has limited adaptive, social-communication, and play skills. She spends most of her time in daycare flapping her hands. She attends daycare after receiving early intervention services in her home in the mornings. How can the daycare workers reduce Sheila's stereotypic behaviors? Sheila's goal is to complete developmentally appropriate fine motor activities (e.g., picking up toys, manipulating toys, etc.) as a replacement for hand flapping approximately 75% of the time.

Empirically Supported Treatment Choices

No treatments have been identified by both the NAC and Wong et al. (2014) for systematic reviews for young children like Sheila. Behavioral interventions (antecedent-based intervention, differential reinforcement, extinction, functional behavioral assessment, reinforcement, response interruption and redirection, and time delay prompts) are research supported for children under 5 years of age based on the Wong et al. (2014) review and these same interventions have been found to be effective for children 3-6 years of age according to the NAC report. Parent training has been found to be effective for reducing stereotypic behavior for children 0-6 years of age according to the NAC, whereas exercise, FCT, social narratives, social skills training, and visual supports were supported for children under 5 years of age (Wong et al., 2014).

Client Variables

In Sheila's case, social narratives were eliminated because they are not appropriate for young children who cannot attend to the story. Regarding Sheila's intensive behavior, therapists have reported that the function (i.e., purpose) of Sheila's hand flapping is automatic reinforcement. In Sheila's case, hand flapping produces a physiological sensation that is pleasant.

Context Variables

Daycare setting. Most children spend a minimum of 15-36 hours a week in the care of someone other than parents (Laughlin, 2013). The rising prevalence of children with ASD not only means there is an increase in children attending daycare, but also an increase in the number of daycare staff that will be responsible for interacting with and serving these young children. Young children with ASD attending daycare are more likely to be successful in these settings if their childcare providers receive training in how to use ESTs. However, the demographic profile of daycare staff suggests there are significant challenges with developing a feasible training model. According to the U.S. Bureau of Labor Statistics, the median income for a childcare worker is approximately $20,000 and the educational requirements are a high school diploma or early childhood certificate. Thus, the majority of daycare staff are not well paid and enter the workforce under-trained, which means turnover rates are bound to soar in the future (Whitebook & Sakai, 2003). Given the difficulty many children with ASD experience with unexpected change (American Psychiatric Association, 2013), high turnover will reasonably be associated with even greater difficulty with attaining, maintaining, and generalizing skills. Further, when turnover is high and skill sets of the many daycare workers may be limited, daycare directors may question the value of training staff members to use complicated ESTs. However, directors may see the value in securing the training if daycare workers receive training on those ESTs that require low response effort and are equally effective with other children who engage in disruptive behavior (i.e., are effective with children not diagnosed with ASD). In addition, EB practitioners will want to emphasize to daycare directors that turnover is less likely when staff have the skill sets needed to perform their jobs (Whitebook, 1989).

Other contextual variables. The practitioner discussed the list of ESTs selected as appropriate for Sheila with her parents and the daycare director. Sheila's parents liked the idea of receiving behavioral parent training. The behavioral parent training methods have also been used to train teachers (Brookman-Frazee et al., 2012). The director reported that time out, a common behavioral strategy, was used in the daycare. Several of the remaining treatment options were considered too complex for the staff to use (e.g., FCT and social skills training). Exercise was not considered a good fit for Sheila because of the daycare's staffing schedules. Specifically, it would be too complicated to arrange exercise for just one child and too challenging to schedule exercise for multiple children given the small number of staff and relatively frequent staff absence from the workplace. Although all parties considered visual schedules acceptable, they agreed it would be too hard to start using the behavioral parent training strategies and the visual schedules at the same time. Everyone agreed visual schedules might be considered after behavioral parent training strategies was consistently being used in both settings.

Integrating Client and Contextual Variables into Treatment

Three behavioral/parent training strategies were taught to both Sheila's parents and the daycare staff. These include: effective instruction delivery (EID), time in, and reinforcement for appropriate behavior (i.e., differential reinforcement for behaviors other than stereotypic behavior). EID, time-in, and reinforcement are associated with improved outcomes for children with ASD but they overlap considerably with the compliance literature involving children who engage in high rates of disruptive behavior (Brookman-Frazee, Stahmer, Baker-Ericzen, & Tsai, 2012). In addition, the response interruptions and redirection strategy (RIRD; Sanai, Gregory, Uran, & Fantetti, 2015) was deemed important because they all believed they needed a strategy to use when she started flapping her hands.

Effective instruction delivery (EID). Most adults do not deliver clear and easily understood instructions to children but they can be taught to do so (Dufrene, Parker, Menousek, Zhou, Harpole, & Olmi, 2012; Shriver & Allen, 1997; Stephenson & Hanley 2010). EID involves securing the child's attention, being in close proximity to the child, delivering commands that are descriptive and directive, using a neutral authoritative tone, and waiting for the child's response before prompting. EID is critical for increasing child compliance (Dufrene et al., 2012; Everett, Olmi, Edwards, & Tingstrom, 2005; Matheson & Shriver, 2005). Although these studies largely reflect teacher-student interactions in the context of elementary schools, it shows that EID can be used effectively to increase compliance when there is a large adult-to-child ratio in a setting. In addition, adults working with preschool-aged children are able to quickly acquire EID skills (Mandal, Olmi, Edwards, Tingstrom, & Benoit, 2000), suggesting extensive training would not be necessary.

An examination of the components of EID shows concordance with discrete trial training (DTT), one of the most effective methods for teaching young children with ASD like Sheila (Lovaas, 1987). With DTT, the daycare staff delivers an instruction that is brief, clear, and descriptive enough to produce to the desired outcome (e.g., "Play with these blocks, Sheila"). In addition, the component of using a neutral tone may be particularly relevant to young children with ASD because using a tone that is too harsh or too passive may evoke an emotional response (Whittingham, Sofronoff, Sheffield, & Sanders, 2009), thus decreasing the probability of compliance. Finally, by avoiding "rapid firing" of instructions (i.e., multiple iden-tical commands in quick succession), daycare staff working with Sheila are likely to see increases in compliance because young children with ASD are less confused by unnecessary verbal stimuli (Lovaas, Koegel, & Schreibman, 1979). Because EID can be quickly taught, and is effective with both children with ASD and the general population of young children, it is an ideal intervention strategy to teach Sheila's daycare staff.

Time-in. Although time-out is a commonly used disciplinary practice and can be used effectively for some children, it can be counter-productive for children with ASD. For example, some young children with ASD seek social isolation, a critical component of a time-out procedure. In addition, children with ASD can often engage in stereotypic behavior after an adult puts them in time-out. Thus, they may be inadvertently reinforcing Sheila's hand flapping when the daycare staff uses time-out as a consequence. An alternative to the reactive intervention of time-out, time-in is an antecedent intervention that includes the delivery of attention that is contingent on socially appropriate behavior (Roberts, Tingstrom, Olmi, & Bellipanni, 2008). This attention may come in the form of giving Sheila verbal praise, smiles, or physical contact (e.g., hug, high five, gentle touch on the arm, etc.) and aims to provide a rich schedule of reinforcement when appropriate behavior is displayed (Roberts et al., 2008). For example, when Sheila watches other kids, smiles at other people, or follows instructions, time-in should be delivered. Time-in, in combination with EID, has been shown to be effective in gaining compliance in children with behavior problems (Ford, Olmi, Edwards, & Tingstrom, 2001; Mandal et al., 2000) and developmental delays (Benoit, Edwards, Olmi, Wilczynski, & Mandal, 2001).

Child-directed play (i.e., allowing the child to be in charge of the "rules" of play and the adult simply follows the child's lead in appropriate play activities), can be an important part of time-in. Sheila's play skills are limited so when she picks up a toy or manipulates the buttons on an electronic device, her daycare workers can say, "I like the way you are playing with that toy, Sheila." Given the fact that Sheila attends a good daycare that already delivers a high degree of social attention to Sheila, time-in should be a natural fit for the daycare setting. Training of daycare staff in the use of time-in would focus on ensuring that delivery of social attention occurs when Sheila engages in appropriate behavior. In short, time-in can effectively increase compliance for all young children, so it would be a valuable skill for all daycare staff to develop.

Reinforcement. Positive contingent consequences would involve giving Sheila positive attention, a preferred object, or fun activity when she uses her hands in a non-stereotypic manner. The daycare staff may need to tell Sheila to play with a specific toy. For decades, children have responded more effectively to adult instruction when given contingent praise (Schutte & Hopkins, 1970; Wolf, Risley, & Mees, 1963). It is noteworthy that delivery of positive contingent consequences is the cornerstone of intensive behavioral treatment for ASD by trained therapists and has also been used effectively by parents and teachers to increase compliance in children with ASD (Bellipanni, Tingstrom, Olmi, & Roberts, 2013; Everett et al., 2005). The daycare staff could consult with Sheila's parents to identify highly reinforcing toys or activities that could be incorporated into her day when she is using her hands appropriately.

Response Interruption/Redirection (RIRD). RIRD is an intervention in which children with ASD are prevented from engaging in the problem behavior and told to demonstrate a behavior that is incompatible with stereotypic behavior (e.g., hand-flapping). It is an appropriate treatment for automatically reinforced behavior. When a stereotypic motor action occurs, an adult delivers an instruction that the client demonstrate an incompatible motor action (e.g., pick up that toy and hand it to me; Sanai et al, 2015). In Sheila's case, the daycare staff could encourage her to play with a ball or toy rather than hand flapping. Sheila's daycare workers were encouraged to use this method instead of time-out as a consequence for hand flapping. For other children, time out can be retained at the discretion of the daycare director.

Final Steps of Evidence-Based Practice

Despite the fact that the treatments selected for these examples have been shown to be effective and are a good match based on both client and contextual variables, no treatment will be effective if the staff do not receive training that allows them to develop and accurately implement the ESTs. Individuals implementing behavioral strategies should be trained using strategies that include not only instruction, but also constructive feedback (Lerman, Vorndran, Addison, & Kuhn, 2004). In addition, behavioral skills training (i.e., providing instruction followed by repeated modeling, practice, and feedback) have been effectively used to increase the use of behavioral methods with childcare workers (Hine, 2014).

EB practitioners should also collect data to determine if the treatment is effective and if the interventions selected remain a good contextual fit for the setting. For the examples in the current article, alternative interventions must be considered if Jamie's play interactions with other peers do not increase and Sheila's hand flapping does not decrease. Further, consumer satisfaction data should be collected from the individuals who are responsible for implementing the ESTs. Barriers frequently emerge when ESTs are transferred from research conditions to real world settings (e.g., Montessori schools and daycares). EB practitioner can resolve these real world challenges only if they maintain a dialogue with key stakeholders (e.g., Montessori teachers, daycare directors and staff, parents). For example, if the daycare director is concerned that staff turnover has meant that they have had to pay repeatedly for staff training, the parents may offer to pay for the training, or some of the training could be web-based if feasible. Implementing ESTs can seem daunting when considering all of the client and contextual variables that must be considered after being familiar with the scientific evidence. But by using the evidence-based practice model for decision-making, EP practitioners can systematically eliminate treatments that are not best suited for each client in every unique setting and then identify those ESTs that are a good fit.

Author's note:

A special thanks to Karen Wilczynski who reviewed parts of this manuscript to ensure a good contextual fit for Montessori schools. The first author thanks Leland Boren and the Plassman Family for their support of the Center for Autism Spectrum Disorder at Ball State University. They have all inspired creative approaches to solving challenges for individuals with ASD and other disabilities. Correspondence concerning this article should be addressed to Susan M. Wilczynski, PhD, BCBA-D, Plassman Family Distinguished Professor, Ball State University, Department of Special Education, Muncie, IN 47306. Email: smwilczynski@bsu.edu.

References

Al, S., Sari, R. M., & Kahya, N. C. (2012). A different perspective on education: Montessori and Montessori school architecture. *Procedia-Social and Behavioral Sciences, 46,* 1866-1871.

American Psychiatric Association. (2013). *Diagnostic and Statistical Manual of Mental Disorders* (5th ed.). Arlington, VA: American Psychiatric Publishing.

Ansari, A., & Winsler, A. (2014). Montessori public school pre-K programs and the school readiness of low-income Black and Latino children. *Journal of Educational Psychology, 106*(4), 1-14.

Bellipanni, K. D., Tingstrom, D. H., Olmi, D. J., & Roberts, D. S. (2013). The sequential introduction of positive antecedent and consequent components in a compliance training package with elementary students. *Behavior Modification*, doi: 10.1177/0145445513501959

Benoit, D. A., Edwards, R. P., Olmi, D. J., Wilczynski, S. M., & Mandal, R. L. (2001). Generalization of a positive treatment package for child noncompliance. *Child & Family Behavior Therapy, 23*(2), 19-32.

Brookman-Frazee, L, Stahmer, A., Baker-Ericzen, M. J., & Tsai, K. (2006) Parenting interventions for children with autism spectrum and disruptive behavior disorders: Opportunities for cross-fertilization. *Clinical Child and Family Psychological Review, 9* (3-4), 181-200.

Dufrene, B. A., Parker, K., Menousek, K., Zhou, Q., Harpole, L.H., & Olmi, J. (2012). Direct behavioral consultation in Head Start to increase teacher use of praise and effective instruction delivery. *Journal of Educational and Psychological Consultation, 22,* 159-186.

Everett, G. E., Olmi, D. J., Edwards, R. P., & Tingstrom, D. H. (2005). The contributions of eye contact and contingent praise to effective instruction delivery in compliance training. *Education and Treatment of Children 28*(1), 48-62.

Ford, A. D., Olmi, D. J., Edwards, R. P., & Tingstrom, D. H. (2001). The sequential introduction of compliance training components with elementary-aged children in general education classroom settings. *School Psychology Quarterly, 16*, 142-157.

Hart, B. M., & Risley, T. R. (1968). Establishing use of descriptive adjectives in the spontaneous speech of disadvantaged preschool children. *Journal of Applied Behavior Analysis, 1*(2), 109.

Hart, B., & Risley, T. R. (1975). Incidental teaching of language in the preschool. *Journal of Applied Behavior Analysis, 8*(4), 411-420.

Hine, K. (2014). Effects of behavioral skills training with directed data collection on the acquisition of behavioral practices by workers in a private, not-for-profit child care center. *Journal of Organizational Behavior Management, 34*(3), 223-232. doi:10.1080/01608061.2014.944744

Jones, J., Lerman, D. C., & Lechago, S. (2014). Assessing stimulus control and promoting generalization via video modeling when teaching social responses to children with autism. *Journal of Applied Behavior Analysis, 47*(1), 37-50.

Laughlin, L. (2013). *Who's minding the kids? Child care arrangements: Spring 2011.* Current Population Reports, P70-135. Washington, DC: US Census Bureau.

Lerman, D. C., Vorndran, C. M., Addison, L., & Kuhn, S. C. (2004). Preparing teachers in evidence-based practices for young children with autism. *School Psychology Review, 33*(4), 510.

Lovaas, O. I., Koegel, R. I., & Schreibman, L. (1979). Stimulus overselectivity in autism: A review of research. *Psychological Bulletin, 86*(6), 1236-1254.

Lovaas, O. I. (1987). Behavioral treatment and normal educational and intellectual functioning in young autistic children. *Journal of Consulting and Clinical Psychology, 55*(1), 3-9.

Mandal. R. L., Olmi, D. J., Edwards, R. P., Tingstrom, D. H., & Benoit, D. A. (2000). Effective instruction delivery and time-in: Positive procedures for achieving child compliance. *Child and Family Behavior Therapy, 22*, 1-12.

Matheson, A. S., & Shriver, M. D. (2005). Training teachers to give effective commands: Effects on student compliance and academic behaviors. *School Psychology Review, 34*(2), 202 - 219.

McGee, G. G., Almeida, M. C., Sulzer-Azaroff, B., & Feldman, R. S. (1992). Promoting reciprocal interactions via peer incidental teaching. *Journal of Applied Behavior Analysis, 25*(1), 117-126.

McKenzie, G. K., & Zascavage, V. S. (2012). Montessori instruction: A model for inclusion in early childhood classrooms. *Montessori Life: A Publication of the American Montessori Society, 24* (1), 32-38.

McLay, L., Carnett, A., van der Meer, L., & Lang, R. (2015). Using a video Modeling-Based Intervention package to toilet train two children with Autism. *Journal of Developmental and Physical Disabilities,* 1-21

Miltenberger, C. A., & Charlop, M. H. (2015). The comparative effectiveness of portable video modeling vs. traditional video modeling interventions with children with autism spectrum disorders. *Journal of Developmental and Physical Disabilities, 27*(3), 341-358.

National Autism Center. (2015). Findings and conclusions: National standards project, phase 2. Randolph, MA.

National Professional Development Center on Autism Spectrum Disorder. (2014). *Evidence-Based Practices.* Retrieved from http://autismpdc.fpg.unc.edu/evidence-based-practices

Roberts, D. S., Tingstrom, D. H., Olmi, D. J., & Bellipanni, K. D. (2008). Positive antecedent and consequent components in child compliance training. *Behavior modification, 32*(1), 21-38.

Rudy, N. A., Betz, A. M., Malone, E., Henry, J. E., & Chong, I. M. (2014). Effects of video modeling on teaching bids for joint attention to children with autism. *Behavioral Interventions, 29*(4), 269-285.

Ryan, C. S., Hemmes, N. S., Sturmey, P., Jacobs, J. D., & Grommet, E. K. (2008). Effects of a brief staff training procedure on instructors' use of incidental teaching and students' frequency of initiation toward instructors. *Research in Autism Spectrum Disorders, 2*(1), 28-45.

Sanai, V., Gregory, M. K., Uran, K. J., & Fantetti, M. A. (2015). Parametric analysis of response interruptions and redirection as treatment for stereotypy. *Journal of Applied Behavior Analysis, 48,* 96-106

Schutte, R. C., & Hopkins, B.L. (1970). The effects of teacher attention on following instructions in a kindergarten class. *Journal of Applied Behavior Analysis, 3,* 117-122.

Shriver, M. D., & Allen, K. D. (1997). Defining child noncompliance: An examination of temporal parameters. *Journal of Applied Behavior Analysis, 30,* 173-176

Slocum, T. A., Detrich, R., Wilczynski, S. M., Spencer, T. D., Lewis, T., & Wolfe, K. (2014). The evidence-based practice of applied behavior analysis. *The Behavior Analysts, 37*(1), 41-56.

Stephenson, K. M., & Hanley, G. P. (2010). Preschooler's compliance with simple instructions: A descriptive and experimental evaluation. *Journal of Applied Behavior Analysis, 43,* 229-247.

Whitebook, M. (1989). Research report: Who cares? Child care teachers and the quality of care in America. *Young Children, 45*(1), 41-45.

Whitebook, M., & Sakai, L. (2003). Turnover begets turnover: An examination of job and occupational instability among child care center staff. *Early Childhood Research Quarterly, 18*(3), 273-293.

Whittingham, K., Sofronoff, K., Sheffield, J., & Sanders, M. R. (2009). Stepping Stones Triple P: an RCT of a parenting program with parents of a child diagnosed with an Autism Spectrum Disorder. *Journal of Abnormal Child Psychology, 37*(4), 469-480.

Wolf, M., Risley, T., & Mees, H. (1963). Application of operant conditioning procedures to the behaviour problems of an autistic child. *Behaviour Research and Therapy, 1*(2), 305-312.

Wong, C., Odom, S. L., Hume, K. A., Cox, A. W., Fettig, A., Kucharczyk, S.,…Schultz, T.R. (2015). Evidence-based practices for children, youth, and young adults with autism spectrum disorder: A comprehensive review. *Journal of Autism and Developmental Disorders, 45*(7), 1951-1966.

Combining The Picture Exchange Communication System (PECS) with Functional Communication Training (FCT) to Decrease Problem Behavior in Children with Autism

Chris A. LaBelle, Cathy Jones, Marjorie H. Charlop, and Benjamin R. Thomas

Abstract

Ancillary decreases in the problem behavior of children with autism have been found following the implementation of the Picture Exchange Communication System (PECS). However, no studies used functional analysis (FA) to ascertain behavioral function, nor has the PECS protocol been modified to target functions of problem behaviors other than access to tangibles, using a functional communication training (FCT) format. In the present study, a multiple baseline design across children with an additional reversal control was used to assess the effects of PECS alone and in combination with FCT upon problem behavior. Following FA baselines, each child was taught PECS, presented with FCT using PECS, then presented with reversal, and finally presented with FCT again. Results suggested that the children's problem behavior decreased or remained level during PECS training. Further decreases in problem behavior were found during the modified PECS + FCT training. In addition, all of the children's problem behavior increased upon FCT reversal, then decreased upon return to FCT.

Keywords: autism spectrum disorder, picture exchange communication system (PECS), functional communication training (FCT), functional analysis

Children with autism spectrum disorder (ASD) often have significant deficits in a number of communication and social skills (APA, 2013; LaRue, Weiss, & Cable, 2009). Unfortunately, a lack of appropriate communication skills has been associated with an increased risk for engaging in problem behaviors that act as barriers to academic learning, social interaction, and community participation (Dominick, Ornstein-Davis, Lainhart, Tager-Flusberg, & Folstein, 2007; Matson & Nebel-Schwalm, 2007). More than 50% of children with ASD are reported to display severe problem behaviors such as self-injury, aggression, or property destruction (Farmer & Aman, 2010; Lecavalier, 2006). Research increasingly shows that problem behaviors in children with ASD often serve one or more communicative function, often because of deficits in conventional vocal communication (Bowman, Fisher, Thompson, & Piazza, 1997; Day, Horner, & O'Neill, 1994; Carr & Durand, 1985; Durand & Carr, 1992; LaRue et al., 2011; Thomas, Lafasakis, & Sturmey, 2010). Accordingly, remediation of problem behavior and related communication training are critical components of behavioral and developmental interventions for children with ASD (Robertson, 2015; Weitlauf et al., 2014).

Addressing problem behaviors begins with functional behavior assessment (FBA), which is considered the standard practice and is a process that gathers information concerning contextual antecedents that evoke problem behavior, and the consequences that maintain it (Durand & Merges, 2001; Sturmey, 1995). Functional analysis (FA) procedures are forms of FBA that use an experimental approach, and are considered best practice for assessing problem behavior in children with ASD (Wong et al., 2015). This type of approach is beneficial because when children with ASD engage in problem behavior, their communication deficits can make it challenging to tell others what is upsetting them (Thomas, Lafasakis, & Sturmey, 2010). Similarly, it can sometimes be difficult for others to understand why problem occurs when observing the child behave (Hanley, 2012). Therefore, using FA procedures can help determine the purpose or communicative function of problem behavior for children with ASD (Carr & Durand, 1985; Hagopian, Fisher, Thompson, Owen- De Schryver, Iwata, & Wacker, 1997; LaRue et al., 2011).

In general, FA procedures involve arranging situations that may be more or less likely to bring about problem behavior, to reveal functional relationships (e.g., Hanley 2012; Iwata, Dorsey, Slifer, Bauman, & Richman, 1982/1994). There are several possible environmental relationships that are typically explored in FA. For example, some children might engage in problem behavior to gain access to preferred tangible items such as toys or food. In FA, this relationship is assessed by observing differences in problem behavior when a child interacts with preferred items, compared to interrupting or denying access to the activities (i.e., told "No," or time to "Clean up toys"). Other children may use problem behavior as a means to escape difficult activities such as household chores, academic tasks, or some social games (Iwata et al., 1982/1994). To assess this relationship, differences in problem behavior are compared during the presence and absence of task demands. Conversely, social interaction might be motivating and therefore problem behavior can function to gain attention from others (Carr & Durand, 1985). In sum, different children with ASD might engage in problem behavior for different reasons. Thus, using FA can help individualize the treatment approach. Additionally, FA results can serve as a guide for creating communication treatments that specifically apply when the functions of problem behaviors are revealed to be communicative in intent (Falcomata, White, Muething, & Fragale, 2012; Sigafoos, Arthur, & O'Reilly, 2003; Sturmey, 1995).

Functional communication training (FCT) is a behavior analytic procedure that begins with an FA to ascertain communicative function, and then teaches communication responses that specifically match the identified functions as replacement behaviors (Carr & Durand, 1985; Tiger, Hanley, & Bruzek, 2008). That is, the trained communication response is intended to evoke the exact same reinforcers as the problem behaviors(s) targeted for reduction (e.g., asking for a "break" when the child values escaping demands; Durand, 1990). Thus, FCT is an individualized procedure that can address various possible functions of a child's problem behavior, such as escaping demands, accessing activities or rituals, or gaining attention, and even those behaviors that have multiple functions (Carr & Durand, 1985; Day et al., 1994; Falcomata et al., 2012; Hagopian, Fisher, Sullivan, Acquisto & LeBlanc, 1998; LaRue et al., 2011). FCT may involve various communication modalities, depending on the preference or skill set of the child in training (e.g., spoken words, card touch, manual sign, etc.; LaRue et al., 2009; Tiger et al., 2008).

Similar to FCT, The Picture Exchange Communication System (PECS) is an evidenced-based program that teaches communication behavior (Charlop-Christy, Carpenter, Le, LeBlanc, & Kellet, 2002; Weitlauf et al., 2014; Wong et al., 2015). PECS was developed specifically to teach simple non-vocal communication skills to children with speech and language disorders, including those with ASD (Bondy & Frost, 1994). PECS training involves teaching individuals to request desired tangible items such as toys, activities, and foods by giving pictures of those items to another person, rather than speaking (Frost & Bondy, 2002). The first step to PECS training, therefore, is conducting a preference assessment to find out the items or activities a child might be motivated to request. This is usually done by observing a child and documenting what s/he interacts with most often. Next, the several preferred items are arranged in front of the child and those selected most often are used for training (Bondy & Frost, 1994). During training, a therapist prompts the child to give a picture to another person that corresponds to a preferred item (Greenberg, Tomaino, & Charlop, 2014). Once the picture is exchanged, the child is then given the item (Bondy & Frost, 1994). For example, if a child likes drinking juice, the training session might involve teaching the child to give a picture of a juice box to a person who will in turn, give the child an actual juice box to drink. Therefore, the process of PECS training involves focusing on manding and the motivational and social aspects of speech. There is considerable empirical support for using PECS to increase the communication skills of individuals with ASD and related communication deficits (Ganz, Davis, Lund, Goodwyn, & Simpson, 2012; Hart & Banda, 2010; Lerna, Esposito, Conson, & Massagli, 2014; Schreibman & Stahmer, 2014; Sulzer-Azaroff, Hoffman, Horton, Bondy, & Frost, 2009). It has even been shown to lead to or facilitate vocal speech (Carr & Felce, 2006; Greenberg, Tomaino, & Charlop, 2014; Schreibman, & Stahmer, 2014).

The relationship of PECS acquisition to reductions in problem behavior has been less studied (Battaglia & McDonald, 2015). To date, only a small collection of studies on PECS have reported reductions in problem behavior in addition to increases in targeted communication skills (Buckley & Newchok, 2005; Charlop-Christy, et al., 2002; Charlop, Malmberg, & Berquist, 2008; Frea, Arnold, & Vittimberga, 2001). Despite the promising effects on problem behavior, the current PECS literature does not include FA to ascertain communicative function of the participants' problem behaviors prior to training. Instead, the PECS protocol involves assessing children's preferences, and then teaching children to request those preferred tangible items. Therefore, the effects of PECS training on problem behaviors that serve other communicative functions (e.g., escape or attention) is largely unknown. Relatedly, motivation for these consequences might have simply been absent in the PECS training paradigm, but could likely emerge during a typical behavior intervention session. Thus, the effects of PECS use on problem behavior outside of a PECS training context also warrants further exploration.

Accordingly, PECS training appears to be beneficial for increasing communication in many children and reducing problem behavior in some children; however, the paradigm warrants further exploration on its effectiveness in relation to results of FA for problem behavior. The purpose of the present study therefore was to evaluate the effectiveness of PECS training in relation to results of FA for problem behavior. First, we conducted FA for all participants in baseline to determine functions of problem behaviors. Following FA, each child was taught the standard use of PECS for requesting preferred items, regardless of behavioral function, and its effect on problem behavior was assessed. Finally, PECS was combined with the FCT paradigm to specifically address multiple maintaining functions of problem behavior, and its effects on problem behavior were compared to the standard PECS training protocol in a typical behavioral intervention context.

Method

Participants and Setting

Three children diagnosed with ASD by two independent agencies participated in this study. All children attended weekly behavior intervention sessions and were selected for this study because they exhibited minimal or no vocal communication and also exhibited high frequencies of problem behaviors. All of the children's problem behaviors interfered with their treatment progress and participation in their classrooms (see Table 1).

Erica was a 5-year, 1-month old female and had minimal vocalizations. She imitated one or two word phrases when asked to do so, but rarely used spontaneous speech. Erica displayed poor self-help skills (e.g., she was not toilet trained) and engaged in high rates of ritualistic behavior. Erica displayed some stereotypic behaviors including feeling textures, smelling objects, tapping and spinning objects, and hand flapping. Erica frequently exhibited disruptive behavior including grabbing, aggression, and climbing on furniture during intervention sessions.

Henry was a 5-year, 2-month old male who did not have functional communication, although occasionally made attempts to vocally imitate models (e.g., making mouth movements) when desired objects were held in front of him. Henry had poor self-help skills and engaged in stereotypic and ritualistic play. Henry engaged in high rates of stereotypic behaviors including finger twirling and head rolling.

Sam was a 4-year, 3-month old male who did not have spontaneous or imitative speech. Sam displayed poor self-help skills (e.g., he was not toilet trained) and engaged in stereotypic and ritualistic behavior. Sam's stereotypy was primarily exhibited in a monotone vowel sound frequently emitted while Sam covered his ears. Sam was frequently non-compliant and repeatedly got out of his seat during intervention sessions. When Sam eloped, he rolled around on the floor, and/or attempted to run away.

All phases of the present study were conducted in 2.9m by 2.9m intervention rooms equipped with one-way mirrors so that experimenters could observe and record data. The rooms contained a table, two chairs, and toys that were displayed, but out of the child's reach. Two therapists were also present: one person acting as the primary therapist who provided instructions and consequences, and another to prompt the participants' requests during the communication training phases (i.e., the shadow).

Materials

Prior to FA and implementation of PECS and PECS/FCT training, experimenters conducted informal assessments of preferred items by asking the children's parents and therapists about favorite edibles and toys, as well as observing the children's choices during free play. In addition, experimenters conducted formal preference tests to determine the items used during PECS training, according to the PECS training manual (Frost & Bondy, 1994). The preference assessments involved presenting five to eight items identified during observation, and then noting the child's order of selection relative to the available items. The first item selected by the child was removed from the array after brief interaction, and set aside for training. Next, the child was given an opportunity to make a selection from the remaining items. This procedure was repeated until the child selected three to five items, and these "preferred" items were used for PECS training.

FA and PECS/FCT materials. The tasks presented to the children during FA conditions, and all PECS/FCT (e.g., training, reversal, and maintenance), were similar to the tasks that were routinely presented during intervention sessions in their behavior management program. Tasks for Erica included following simple commands, turn taking, and pronouncing one-word requests. Tasks for Henry included verbal and non-verbal imitation, receptive labeling of objects, letters, and numbers, and understanding of prepositions. Tasks for Sam included verbal and non-verbal imitation, understanding of prepositions, and receptively identifying body parts. No tasks were presented during the alone or play conditions.

PECS materials. Each child was provided with a PECS book containing a sentence strip and a minimum of 10 one-inch picture cards for desired items. Erica's book contained an "I want" card as well as an "I see" card, whereas Henry's and Sam's books contained "I want" cards as well as "Yes" and "No" cards. Some cards were photocopied from the *Picture Communication Symbols Combination Book* (Mayer-Johnson, 1994) and other cards were constructed by incorporating the food packaging or advertisements for the item as recommended by Frost and Bondy (1994).

Research Design

A multiple baseline design across children with a reversal (Baer, Wolf, & Risley, 1968) was used to assess the effects of PECS alone and combining PECS with FCT on problem behavior. In baseline, a multi-element design is embedded for each participant according to analogue FA procedures (Barlow & Hayes, 1979; Iwata et al., 1982/1994).

Dependent Measures

The dependent measures for Erica, Henry, and Sam are defined in Table 1. The presence and absence of dependent variables were measured within consecutive 10-second intervals, using a partial-interval recording system. Dividing the number of intervals containing target behaviors by the total number of intervals observed and multiplying by 100 calculated percentage occurrence. For each session, the first 10 minutes were scored. For Erica and Henry, all of the sessions were scored. For Sam, all FA, FCT, and reversal sessions were scored, but only every third PECS training session was scored due to his extensive number of training sessions.

Table 1:
Operational Definitions of Problem Behaviors for Each Child

Participant	Dependent Measure	Operational Definition
Erica	*Disruptive Behavior*	Flopping and rolling on the floor, hiding under the table, or leaning in her chair and tipping/falling to floor. Hitting, scratching, grabbing, and throwing items.
Henry	*Stereotypic Behavior*	Rotating his head from side to side and gazing up at the ceiling. Looking at his hands while repetitively moving (twirling) his fingers.
Sam	*Elopement*	Moving more than 3ft away from the seat of his chair without being told to do so, or moving the same distance away from a therapist when instructed to sit down.

Procedures

Baseline. Baseline consisted of conducting an analogue FA, largely based upon the Iwata et al. (1982/1994) protocol, and included attention, tangible, escape, and play (control) conditions. Henry's stereotypy was also examined during an alone condition, without access to toys or attention, to confirm or rule-out automatic reinforcement as a possible maintaining function. All FA sessions were 10 minutes in length, and contingent upon problem behavior, access to escape, attention, and tangibles lasting 30 seconds.

PECS training. All of the children were taught the first four phases of PECS for requesting, according to *The Picture Exchange Communication System (PECS): Training Manual* (Frost & Bondy, 1994). During PECS training, participants were taught to mand by exchanging cards that depicted favorite tangible items and activities, according to preference tests in the PECS training protocol. Thus, the cards (mands) did not necessarily correspond to functions of the children's problem behavior as obtained during baseline FA. For example, FA indicated Erica's problem behavior was maintained by attention, tangibles, and escape from demands, however, her PECS cards only depicted preferred tangible objects (edibles and toys). Training sessions lasted between 10 and 30 minutes, and criterion for acquisition in each phase was eight correct responses out of ten opportunities.

PECS/FCT. The experimenters trained each child to exchange cards that matched the functions maintaining their problem behavior, as suggested by FA in baseline. Training took place in the context of a typical intervention session (e.g., completing tasks as described above). Each training trial occurred upon the initiation of each instance of a target behavior (rather than reaching for an item). At this point, the shadowing therapist prompted the child to pick up the PECS card, place it on a sentence strip, and hand it to the primary therapist, as outlined in PECS phase 4 (Frost & Bondy, 2002). Similar to FA sessions, participants were given 30 seconds of access to the requested consequence (e.g., 30 s of rest for a "Break" request). Experimenters taught each mand individually, until participants met criteria of least eight out of ten trials without prompts, before teaching the next functional mand. All PECS/FCT training sessions lasted between 10 and 30 minutes.

Erica's disruptive behavior was found to be multiply controlled and therefore she was taught to mand for attention ("Pay attention to me"), escape from demands (exchanging a "Break" card), and tangibles (toys or edibles). Upon instances of grabbing, for example, once Erica gave the sentence strip containing the "attention" card to the primary therapist, that therapist picked Erica up and spun her around the room for 30 seconds. At the end of the 30 seconds, she was guided back to her seat.

FA indicated Henry's stereotypy was primarily maintained by automatic positive reinforcement. Therefore, he was trained to mand for objects that provided similar non-social sensory consequences to his stereotypy as determined through prior assessment (Piazza et al., 1998), but were considered socially appropriate. For example, his PECS cards contained toys such as a flashlight and a view-master that provided light to gaze at, similar to the light viewed when Henry rolled his head and gazed at the lights in the ceiling. In addition, his PECS cards also contained toys that required hand and finger manipulation such as playing with a koosh ball, plastic letters, and a view-master that had switches to touch with one's fingers.

Sam's eloping behavior was found to be multiply controlled by attention, tangibles, and escape from demands, and thus he was subsequently trained to use PECS to mand for attention (e.g., "Pay attention to me"), and escape from demands (exchanging a "Break" card).

PECS/FCT Maintenance. Once participants met PECS/FCT criterion for all behavioral functions, (e.g., "Break", "Pay attention to me", and/or tangible requests), behaviors were examined during maintenance sessions in which all PECS/FCT cards were available at the same time. These maintenance sessions were 10 minutes in length and were also conducted in the context of an intervention session. Whenever participants independently exchanged any PECS card (e.g., break, attention, or tangibles), they were given immediate access to that request for 30 seconds.

Reversal. Following PECS/FCT training and maintenance sessions, reversal sessions consisted of participants working in a typical intervention session. However, PECS books were not available in the room for manding behavior. A reversal design is an ethical method for practitioners to analyze whether an intended therapeutic variable actually has some effect on the behavior of interest, or if other variables might have influence (Baer et al., 1968). Therefore, a reversal design was used to determine if the introduction of PECS/FCT (i.e., the independent variable) was responsible for changes in problem behavior. For example, when PECS/FCT is used, problem behavior might diminish. However, if PECS/FCT cards are not available, then problem behavior should increase to similar levels observed in baseline. Similarly, when PECS/FCT is reinstated, problem behavior might diminish again, thus demonstrating an effect of PECS/FCT. Reversals provide an incontrovertible way to know what factors are affecting the problem behaviors in research and applied settings. Each session lasted 10 minutes and participants received praise for on-task behavior.

Interobserver Agreement

Two graduate student observers with extensive coursework in behavior analysis scored the sessions. The primary observer scored 100% of sessions, while the secondary observer independently scored 33% of the sessions distributed across all phases, per participant. Percentage agreement for occurrence/non-occurrence of dependent variables was calculated on an interval-by-interval basis by dividing the number of agreements by the number of agreements plus disagreements, and multiplying by 100. Mean interobserver agreement was 92% (range = 73 to 100%).

Figure 1:

Percentage of intervals with problem behavior for Erica, Henry, and Sam, during FA baseline, PECS training, PECS/FCT training, maintenance sessions, reversal sessions, and return to maintenance sessions.

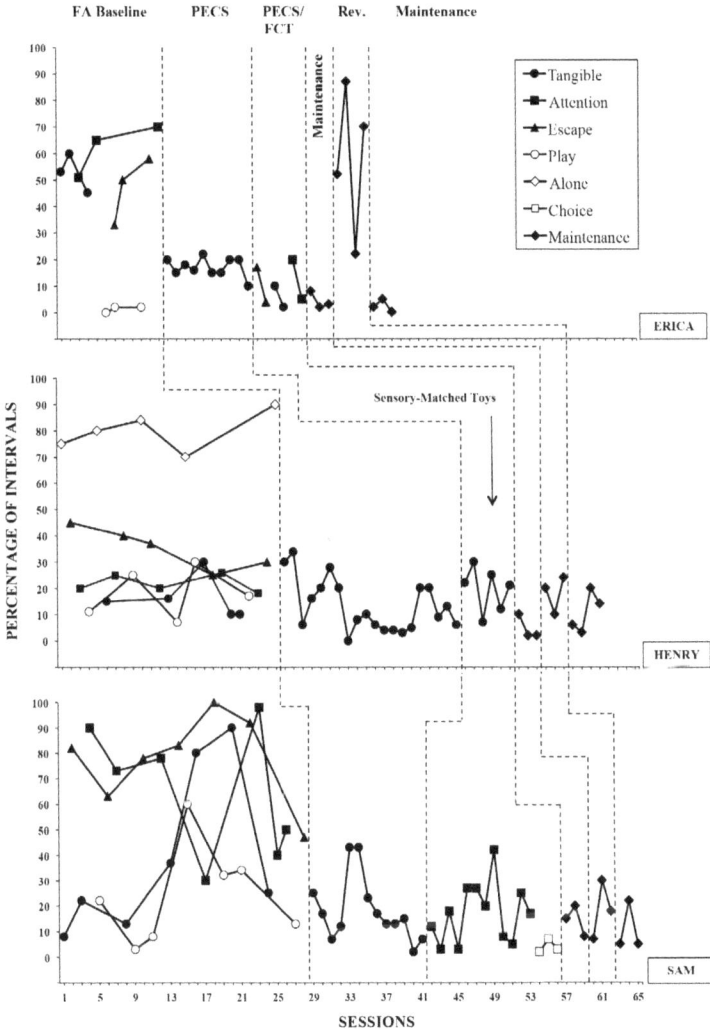

Figure 1. Percentage of intervals with problem behavior for Erica, Henry, and Sam, during FA baseline, PECS training, PECS/FCT training, maintenance sessions, reversal sessions, and return to maintenance sessions.

Results

Figure 1 presents each child's problem behavior during FA baseline, PECS training, FCT, reversal, and maintenance sessions. Below, each child's results are described in order.

Erica's Results

FA baseline. During FA baseline sessions, Erica's problem behavior occurred during an average of 53.9% of the intervals, excluding the play (control) condition (range = 33 to 70%). FA indicated her problem behavior was multiply controlled by attention ($M = 62\%$ of intervals; range = 51 to 70%), tangibles (mean occurrence = 52.7%; range = 45 to 60%), and escape from demands (mean occurrence = 47%; range = 33 to 58%). In contrast, very little disruptive behavior was observed during the play (control) condition ($M = 1.3\%$; range = 0 to 2% of intervals).

PECS training. Erica required 150 total minutes to meet criterion for all PECS phases. Erica's disruptive behavior occurred on average during 17.1% of intervals during each PECS training session in which she requested tangibles (range = 10 to 22%).

PECS/FCT and maintenance. During PECS/FCT, Erica's problem behavior occurred in an average of 7.9% of the intervals overall (range = 2 to 20%). Erica was first taught to mand for escape by exchanging a "Break" card, and problem behavior occurred during an average of 10.5% of intervals for these two sessions (20% then 5%, respectively). Next she exchanged a card to mand for tangibles (similar to traditional PECS), and problem behavior occurred during an average of 6% of the intervals (10% and 2%, respectively). When she was taught to exchange a card to mand for attention, problem behavior was observed during 12.5% of the intervals, on average (20% and then 5%). Finally, Erica's problem behavior further decreased to an average of 4.3% in the three maintenance sessions when all PECS cards were concurrently available (range = 2 to 8% of intervals).

Reversal. During the four reversal sessions, Erica's problem behavior immediately increased to an average of 57.8% of intervals (range = 22 to 87%). This was a slight increase from the occurrence of problem behavior during FA baseline (M = 53.9% of the intervals).

Return to PECS/FCT maintenance. Upon returning to FCT maintenance, Erica's problem behavior decreased to a mean of 2.3% of intervals during three sessions (range = 0 to 5%).

Henry's Results

FA Baseline. Henry emitted stereotypy in an average of 79.8% of intervals during the alone condition sessions (range = 70 to 90%), thus indicating his stereotypy was likely maintained by automatic reinforcement. His stereotypy also occurred in all other baseline FA conditions. The mean occurrence for stereotypy in tangible sessions was 16.2% of intervals (range = 10 to 30%), 21.8% of attention session intervals (range = 18 to 26%), 35.4% of intervals during escape sessions (range = 25 to 45%), and finally during 18% of intervals during the play (control) condition sessions (range = 7 to 30%). Overall, stereotypy occurred during an average of 38.3% of intervals during FA baseline sessions, excluding the play (control) condition (range = 10% in tangible to 90% in the alone condition).

PECS Training. Henry required 300 minutes to meet criterion for all PECS training phases. During PECS training, his stereotypy decreased dramatically across sessions, with an overall mean occurrence of 13.1% of intervals (range = 3 to 30%) when manding for tangibles.

PECS/FCT and maintenance. Henry's stereotypy initially increased during PECS/FCT training, when manding for sensory-matched toys (M = 19.5% of intervals; range = 7 to 30%). However, once Henry met criteria during PECS/FCT, stereotypy decreased to a mean occurrence of 4.7% of the intervals during maintenance sessions (range = 2 to 10%, respectively).

Reversal. When all PECS and PECS/FCT cards were not available to mand for items, and he did not gain access to those items, Henry's stereotypy increased an average of 18% of intervals during the three reversal sessions (range = 10 to 24% of intervals).

Return to PECS/FCT maintenance. Once Henry's PECS/FCT cards and items were available again, his stereotypy then decreased to an average of 10.8% of intervals (range = 3 to 20%).

Sam's Results

FA baseline. Sam displayed problem behavior during an average of 60.9% of intervals, excluding the play (control) condition, in his FA baseline sessions (range = 33 to 70%). Results of his FA indicated that eloping behavior was multiply controlled by attention (M = 65.6% of intervals; range = 30 to 98%), escape from demands (M= 77.9%; range = 47 to 100%), and to a lesser degree access to tangibles (M= 39.3%; range = 8 to 90%). Mean occurrence during the play (control) condition was 24.6% of intervals.

PECS training. Sam required 735 minutes to meet criterion for all PECS phases. Sam's eloping behavior initially decreased within three sessions, followed by a dramatic increase, and then a gradual reduction over the final seven sessions. Overall, eloping occurred during an average of 18.2% of intervals during PECS sessions (range = 2 to 43%, respectively).

PECS/FCT and maintenance. Overall, Sam's eloping behavior occurred during an average of 14.6% of intervals in his PECS/FCT sessions (range = 2 to 43). During sessions in which he manded for attention, Sam averaged 17.3% of intervals with eloping, overall (range = 3 to 43). Initially, eloping occurred very infrequently compared to baseline, however during the fifth session, it began to occur more frequently and variably. Thus, a choice condition was initiated in which a card to mand for attention, escape, and tangible were concurrently available to him (to address all controlling functions of his problem behavior). During this choice condition, Sam's eloping behavior occurred during an average of only 4% of intervals (range = 2 to 7%). Finally, there was a mean occurrence of eloping during 14.3% of intervals in his maintenance sessions (range = 8 to 20%).

Reversal. During his three reversal sessions when manding for attention, escape, (or tangibles) was not available, Sam's overall eloping behavior increased (M =18.3%; range = 7 to 30%).

Return to PECS/FCT Maintenance. When PECS/FCT cards were again available, Sam's eloping behavior decreased again to a frequency substantially below that of baseline occurrence (M = 10.6% of intervals; range = 5 to 22%).

Discussion

In the present study, baseline FA sessions showed frequent problem behaviors across participants and also suggested different and multiple functions for each participant. Next, the children were taught to communicate following the first four phases of the PECS training protocol. All the children successfully acquired PECS to Phase 4, and problem behavior decreased from baseline during PECS training, regardless of problem behavior function. Once children met criteria for PECS training, the children were presented with PECS plus FCT (i.e., PECS/FCT) in which they requested consequences that matched the functions of their problem behaviors during typical intervention session contexts, and this also resulted in substantial decreases in problem behavior. All children's problem behavior increased during the reversal phase, and then decreased again to levels substantially lower than baseline during reimplementation of PECS/FCT in maintenance sessions in which all PECS cards for their respective problem behavior functions were concurrently available.

The results of the present study further support the notion that communication skills and problem behavior are strongly related (Baker, Cantwell, & Mattison, 1980; Carr & Durand, 1985; Funk & Ruppert, 1984; LaRue et al., 2011), and that acquisition of language skills corresponds with reductions in problem behavior (Bowman et al., 1997; Funk & Ruppert, 1984).

The results also indicate that for all three children, the mere training of PECS was associated with a dramatic decrease in problem behavior, regardless of the functions of their behavior. This is consistent with previous literature that also suggested a concomitant decrease in problem behaviors with the use of PECS to increase communication skills (Buckley & Newchok, 2005; Charlop-Christy et al., 2002; Charlop et al., 2008; Frea et al., 2001). However, as previously noted, PECS training sessions do not always reflect natural instructional contexts or address multiple functions; therefore these conditions were assessed further after modifying the PECS protocol to include the FCT paradigm.

During PECS/FCT sessions in typical environments, all of the children in this study ultimately exhibited decreases in problem behavior, similar to or beyond decreases observed during PECS training alone. First, this decrease is noteworthy in that traditional PECS training sessions, unlike FCT sessions, are not typical work sessions for children. Traditional PECS training sessions consist primarily of the children requesting and gaining access to desired tangibles. That is, minimal demands are made of children and attention is rarely withdrawn during PECS training. However, during traditional FCT sessions, children may experience relevant demands and diversion of staff attention that are typical of an intervention session (Carr & Durand, 1985). In the present study, for example, the children's problem behavior may have initially increased during FCT due to the contrast effect between the low demands in the preceding PECS training and the greater demands experienced in PECS/FCT context. Thus, modifying the PECS protocol to include FA and corresponding FCT appears to expand and enhance communication training beyond PECS training alone by involving a variety of typical contexts into training and therefore addressing relevant motivating operations that may relate to problem behavior.

A second general consideration is that modifying the PECS protocol to include FA and FCT appears to have identified and then addressed the multiple and changing functions that were observed for two participants (Day et al., 1994; Falcomatta et al., 2012; LaBelle & Charlop-Christy, 2002; Lalli & Casey, 1996). For example, FA for Erica and Sam indicated their problem behaviors were also maintained by attention and escape from demands. During Erica's PECS/FCT sessions, she was observed to rapidly switch from requesting edibles, toys, breaks, and attention. When Sam was trained to mand for attention during PECS/FCT, the prevalence of his problem behavior was initially comparable to that during PECS training alone, but then occurred more frequently, possibly due to satiation or change in motivation or preference during the intervention session context. In fact, Sam did not meet criteria during PECS/FCT until he was given a choice to request multiple consequences. Thus, allowing for choice allocation between consequences during PECS/FCT may have addressed his relative preferences (e.g., Harding, Wacker, Berg, Winborn-Kemmerer, & Lee, 2009), or real-time changes in establishing and abolishing motivations (Laraway, Snycerski, Michael, & Poling, 2003). Therefore, the additional maintaining functions addressed during the PECS/FCT sessions would not have been pursued in traditional PECS training aimed at teaching requests for tangible items. As noted previously, using FA to identify all relevant functions of problem behavior and incorporating results into PECS training is especially important for children like Erica and Sam, whose problem behavior was maintained by multiple and changing functions (Day et al., 1994; LaBelle & Charlop-Christy, 2002).

Finally, although PECS has been widely used to teach communication to a number of children in educational and clinical settings (Bondy & Battaglini, 1992; Sulzer-Azaroff et al., 2009) only a small number of empirical studies have been conducted on the effectiveness of PECS in relation to reductions in problem behavior (Battaglia & McDonald, 2015; Hart & Banda, 2010). In fact, one recent study indicates that problem behavior may have increased during PECS training (Boesch, Wendt, Subramanian, & Hsu, 2013). The present study contributes to the small body of literature in that it measured related changes in problem behavior, identified maintaining functions of the problem behavior via FA prior to implementing PECS training, as well as modified the PECS training protocol to include FCT for directly targeting multiple functions of problem behavior. The results of this study, therefore, offer promising support for the use of PECS as an effective communicative means to reduce problem behavior, when FA is included and corresponding behavioral functions are explicitly addressed.

There are some limitations and directions for future research worth noting. First, prevalence of problem behavior may have been artificially low during the PECS training protocol because the training context is not similar to typical instruction or daily situations. That is, PECS occurs in a mass-trial format in which the child repeatedly mands for and receives highly preferred items on a continuous reinforcement schedule. As noted earlier, the training protocol may have masked motivation for other functions, or establishing operations for other functions may not have been present. Thus, the reductions in problem behavior in PECS training may be the result of false positives (Mann & Mueller, 2009). Also, we do not have procedural integrity measures to report.

Second, the PECS/FCT training that occurred in a natural intervention context did not mirror FA conditions that manipulate respective motivation for possible functions of problem behavior. That is, FCT mands were selected apriori, and training commenced for specific mands only upon the initiation of problem behavior (rather than antecedent manipulation). For example, therapist interaction is inherent during instruction, and this may have abolished some of Sam's motivation when being taught to mand for attention. If training sessions were preceded by a period of low interaction, Sam may have acquired the attention mand more quickly, and the potential for satiation may have been limited (Rispoli et al., 2011). Future investigations may consider manipulating establishing operations as well as training to specific motivations within everyday contexts.

When making recommendations for practice, it is important to consider the relationship between lack of communication and problem behaviors. Specifically, when using PECS, it is important to note that the benefits of using the standard PECS training protocol can be expanded to address the potential resolution of problem behaviors that occur in various natural settings, and those that occur for reasons other than gaining access to preferred items (i.e., escape and attention).

Following FA, PECS training should match the functions of problem behavior by specifically teaching the child to request those consequences. For example, if FA results indicate that a child screams to avoid instructional sessions, PECS training should teach the child to exchange a communication card that requests for the removal of task demands. Along these lines, children may engage in problem behavior for several reasons, and FA can distinguish the relationships that are problematic. In these situations, teaching requests for tangible items might be contraindicated because the individual needs of the child would not be addressed. For example, if a child sometimes tantrums to prolong play with toys, but presently desires to spend time with a caregiver after being apart for most of the day, requesting a toy would not provide the attention and affection the child is seeking.

PECS training should also be dynamic. As observed in the present study, children's preferences for tangible items and motivations for various other consequences can be constantly in flux across time and context. This suggests that children's interest in items and forms of attention, for example, might change over the course of minutes, hours, or days (see LaBelle & Charlop-Christy, 2002, for an analysis of the changing functions of children's behavior problems during FA). Similarly, not all consequences may have equal value for a child. To this end, FA and PECS training should assess and address the idiosyncratic differences in potential reinforcers to make communication training more expedient. For example, some children may seek specific forms of attention with one practitioner or caregiver, such as being picked up and tossed in the air, but may have strong preference for hugs and cuddling with another person. As both consequences might motivate problem behavior, FA can help determine exactly where and when (and with whom) PECS training should take place. Additionally, FA procedures can be part of the ongoing PECS training process. In this way, practitioners and caregivers can stay current with the child's motivations and optimize training opportunities across various contexts.

Author Note

Correspondence concerning this article should be addressed to Marjorie H. Charlop, Department of Psychology, Claremont McKenna College, 850 Columbia Ave., Claremont, CA 91711-6420.

References

American Psychiatric Association (2013), *Diagnostic and statistical manual of mental disorders* (5th Ed). Arlington, VA. American Psychiatric Publishing.

Baer, D. M., Wolf, M. M., & Risley, T. R. (1968). Some current dimensions of applied behavior analysis. *Journal of Applied Behavior Analysis, 1*, 91-97. doi: 10.1901/jaba.1968.1-91

Baker, L., Cantwell, D. P., & Mattison, R. E. (1980). Behavior problems in children with pure speech disorders and in children with combined speech and language disorders. *Journal of Abnormal Child Psychology, 8*, 245-256.

Barlow, D. H., & Hayes, S. C. (1979). Alternating treatments design: One strategy for comparing the effects of two treatments in a single subject. *Journal of Applied Behavior Analysis, 12*, 199-210. doi: 10.1901/jaba.1979.12-199

Battaglia, D., & McDonald, M. E. (2015). Effects of the picture exchange communication system (PECS) on maladaptive behavior in children with autism spectrum disorders (ASD): A Review of the literature. *Journal of the American Academy of Special Education Professionals, 10*, 8-20.

Boesch, M. C., Wendt, O., Subramanian, A., & Hsu, N. (2013). Comparative efficacy of the Picture Exchange Communication System (PECS) versus a speech-generating device: Effects on requesting skills. *Research in Autism Spectrum Disorders, 7*, 480-493. doi:10.1016/j.rasd.2012.12.002

Bondy, A. S., & Battaglini, K. (1992). Strengthening the home-school-community interface for students with severe disabilities. In S. Christenson & J. C. Conoley (Eds.), *Home-school collaboration: Building a fundamental educational resource* (pp. 1-19). Washington, DC: NASP Publishers.

Bondy, A., & Frost, L. (1994). The picture exchange communication system. *Focus on Autistic Behavior, 9,* 1-19.

Bowman, L. G., Fisher, W. W., Thompson, R. H., & Piazza, C. C. (1997). On the relation of mands and the function of destructive behavior. *Journal of Applied Behavior Analysis, 30,* 251-265. doi: 10.1901/jaba.1997.30-251

Buckley, S. D., & Newchok, D. K. (2005). Differential impact of response effort within a response chain on use of mands in a student with autism. *Research in Developmental Disabilities, 26,* 77–85. doi:10.1016/j.ridd.2004.07.004

Carr, D. & Felce, J. (2007). Brief report: increasing in production of spoken words in some children with autism after PECS teaching to phase III. *Journal of Autism and Developmental Disorders, 37,* 780-787. Doi: 10.1007/s1083-006-0204-0.

Carr, E. G., & Durand, V. M. (1985). Reducing behavior problems through functional communication training. *Journal of Applied Behavior Analysis, 18,* 111-126. doi: 10.1901/jaba.1985.18-111

Charlop-Christy, M. H., Carpenter, M. Le, L., LeBlanc, L. A., & Kellet, K. (2002). Using the Picture Exchange Communication System (PECS) with children with autism: Assessment of PECS acquisition, speech, social- communication behavior, and problem behavior. *Journal of Applied Behavior Analysis, 35,* 213–231. doi: 10.1901/jaba.2002.35-213

Charlop, M. H., Malmberg, D. B., & Berquist, K. L. (2008). An application of the Picture Exchange Communication System (PECS) with children with autism and a visually impaired therapist. *Journal of Developmental and Physical Disabilities, 20,* 509-525. doi: 10.1007/s10882-008-9112-x

Day, H. M., Horner, R. H., & O'Neill, R. E. (1994). Multiple functions of problem behaviors: Assessment and intervention. *Journal of Applied Behavior Analysis, 27,* 279-289. doi: 10.1901/jaba.1994.27-279

Dominick, K. C., Ornstein-Davis, N., Lainhart, J., Tager-Flusberg, H. & Folstein, S. (2007). Atypical behaviors in children with autism and children with a history of language impairment. *Research in Developmental Disabilities, 28,* 145– 162. doi:10.1016/j.ridd.2006.02.003

Durand, V. M. (1990). *Severe behavior problems: A functional communication training approach.* New York: The Guilford Press.

Durand, V. M., & Carr, E. G. (1992). An analysis of maintenance following functional communication training. *Journal of Applied Behavior Analysis, 25*, 777-794. doi: 10.1901/jaba.1992.25-777

Durand, V. M., & Merges, E. (2001). Functional communication training: A contemporary behavior analytic intervention for problem behaviors. *Focus on Autism and Other Developmental Disabilities, 16*, 110-119. doi: 10.1177/108835760101600207

Falcomata, T. S., White, P., Muething, C. S., & Fragale, C. (2012). A functional communication training and chained schedule procedure to treat challenging behavior with multiple functions. *Journal of Developmental and Physical Disabilities, 24*, 529-538. doi: 10.1007/s10882-012-9287-z

Farmer, C. A., & Aman, M. G. (2010). Aggressive behavior in a sample of children with autism spectrum disorders. *Research in Autism Spectrum Disorders, 5*, 317–323. doi: 10.1016/j.rasd.2010.04.014

Frea, W. D., Arnold, C. L., & Vittimberga, G. L. (2001). A demonstration of the effects of augmentative communication on the extreme aggressive behavior of a child with autism within an integrated preschool setting. *Journal of Positive Behavior Interventions, 3*, 194–198. doi: 10.1177/109830070100300401

Frost, L. A., & Bondy, A. S. (1994). *The picture exchange communication system training manual.* Cherry Hill, N.J: Pyramid Educational Consultants, Inc.

Frost, L., & Bondy, A. S. (2002). *The picture exchange communication system training manual.* (2nd ed). Newark, DE: Pyramid Educational Products, Inc.

Funk, J. B., & Ruppert, E. S. (1984). Language disorders and behavioral problems in preschool children. *Developmental and Behavioral Pediatrics, 5*, 357-360.

Ganz, J. B., Davis, J. L., Lund, E. M., Goodwyn, F. D., & Simpson, R. L. (2012). Meta-analysis of PECS with individuals with ASD: Investigation of targeted versus non-targeted outcomes, participant characteristics, and implementation phase. *Research In Developmental Disabilities, 33*, 406-418. doi: 10.1016/j.ridd.2011.09.023

Greenberg, A. L., Tomaino, M. E., & Charlop, M. H. (2014). Adapting the picture exchange communication system to elicit vocalizations in children with autism. *Journal of Developmental And Physical Disabilities, 26*, 35-51. doi: 10.1007/s10882-013-9344-2

Hagopian, L. P., Fisher, W. W., Sullivan, M. T., Acquisto, J., & LeBlanc, L. A. (1998). Effectiveness of functional communication training with and without extinction and punishment: A summary of 21 inpatient cases. *Journal of Applied Behavior Analysis, 31*, 211– 235. doi: 10.1901/jaba.1998.31-211

Hagopian, L. P., Fisher, W. W., Thompson, R. H., Owen- De Schryver, J., Iwata, B. A., & Wacker, D. P. (1997). Toward the development of structured criteria for interpretation of functional analysis data. *Journal of Applied Behavior Analysis, 30*, 313-326. doi: 10.1901/ jaba.1997.30-313

Hanley, G. P. (2012). Functional assessment of problem behavior: Dispelling myths, overcoming implementation obstacles, and developing new lore. *Behavior Analysis in Practice, 5*, 54.

Harding, J. W., Wacker, D. P., Berg, W. K., Winborn-Kemmerer, L., & Lee, J. F. (2009). Evaluation of choice allocation between positive and negative rein-forcement during functional communication training with young children. *Journal of Developmental and Physical Disabilities, 21*, 443-456. doi: 10.1007/ s10882-009-9155-7

Hart, S. L., & Banda, D. R. (2010). Picture Exchange Communication System with individuals with developmental disabilities: A meta-analysis of sin-gle subject studies. *Remedial and Special Education, 31*(6), 476-488. doi: 10.1177/0741932509338354

Iwata, B. A., Dorsey, M. F., Slifer, K. J., Bauman, K. E., & Richman, G. S. (1994). Toward a functional analysis of self-injury. *Journal of Applied Behavior Analysis*, 27, 197–209. doi: 10.1901/jaba.1994.27-197 (Reprinted from Analysis and Intervention in Developmental Disabilities, 2, 3–20, 1982).

LaBelle, C. A., & Charlop-Christy, M. H. (2002). Individualizing functional analysis to assess multiple and changing functions of severe behavior problems in children with autism. *Journal of Positive Behavior Interventions, 4*, 231-241. doi: 10.1177/10983007020040040601

Lalli J. S., & Casey, S. D. (1996). Treatment of multiply controlled problem behavior. *Journal of Applied Behavior Analysis, 29*, 391-395. doi: 10.1901/ jaba.1996.29-391

Laraway, S., Snycerski, S., Michael, J., & Poling, A. (2003). Motivating operations and terms to describe them: Some further refinements. *Journal of Applied Behavior Analysis, 36*, 407-414. doi: 10.1901/jaba.2003.36-407

LaRue, R., Weiss, M. J., & Cable, M. K. (2009). Functional communication training: The role of speech pathologists and behavior analysts in serving students with autism. *The Journal of Speech And Language Pathology – Applied Behavior Analysis, 3*, 164-172. doi: 10.1037/h0100244

LaRue, R. H., Sloman, K. N., Weiss, M. J., Delmolino, L., Hansford, A., Szalony, J.... & Lambright, N. M. (2011). Correspondence between traditional models of functional analysis and a functional analysis of manding behavior. *Research in Developmental Disabilities, 32*, 2449-2457. doi: 10.1016/j.ridd.2011.07.015

Lecavalier, L. (2006). Behavioral and emotional problems in young people with pervasive developmental disorders: Relative prevalence, effects of subject characteristics, and empirical classification. *Journal of Autism and Developmental Disorders, 36,* 1101–1114. doi: 10.1007/s10803-006-0147-5

Lerna, A., Esposito, D., Conson, M., & Massagli, A. (2014). Long-term effects of PECS on social–communicative skills of children with autism spectrum disorders: A follow-up study. *International Journal of Language & Communication Disorders, 49*(4), 478-485. doi:10.1111/1460-6984.12079

Mann, A.J. & Mueller, M.M. (2009). *False positive functional analysis results as a contributor of treatment failure during functional communication training. Education and Treatment of Children, 32,* 121-149.

Matson, J. L., & Nebel-Schwalm, M. (2007). Assessing challenging behaviors in children with autism spectrum disorders: A review. *Research in Developmental Disabilities, 28,* 567–579. doi:10.1016/j.ridd.2006.08.001

Mayer-Johnson (1994). *The Picture Communication Symbols Combination Book.* Solana Beach, CA: Mayer-Johnson Company.

Piazza, C. C., Fisher, W. W., Hanley, G. P., LeBlanc, L. A., Worsdell, A. S, Lindauer, S. E., & Keeney, K. M. (1998). Treatment of pica through multiple analyses of its reinforcing functions. *Journal of Applied Behavior Analysis, 31,* 165-189. doi: 10.1901/jaba.1998.31-165

Rispoli, M., O'Reilly, M., Lang, R., Machalicek, W., Davis, T., Lancioni, G., & Sigafoos, J. (2011). Effects of motivating operations on problem and academic behavior in classrooms. *Journal of Applied Behavior Analysis, 44,* 187-192. doi: 10.1901/jaba.2011.44-187

Robertson, R. E. (2015). The acquisition of problem behavior in individuals with developmental disabilities as a behavioral cusp. *Behavior Modification, 39*(4), 475-495. doi: 10.1177/0145445515572185.

Schreibman, L. E., & Stahmer, A. C. (2014). A randomized trial comparison of the effects of verbal and pictorial naturalistic communication strategies on spoken language for young children with autism. *Journal of Autism and Developmental Disorders, 44,* 1244–1251. doi:10.1007/s10803-013-1972-y

Sigafoos, J., Arthur, M., & O'Reilly, M. (2003). *Challenging behavior and developmental disability.* London: Whurr Publishers.

Sturmey, P. (1995). Analog baselines: A critical review of the methodology. *Research in Developmental Disabilities, 16*(4), 269-284. doi:10.1016/0891-4222(95)00014-E

Sulzer-Azaroff, B., Hoffman, A. O., Horton, C. B., Bondy, A., & Frost, L. (2009). The Picture Exchange Communication System (PECS): What do the data say? *Focus on Autism and Other Developmental Disabilities, 24*, 89-103. doi: 10.1177/1088357609332743

Thomas, B. R., Lafasakis, M., & Sturmey, P. (2010). The effects of prompting, fading, and differential reinforcement on vocal mands in non-verbal preschool children with autism spectrum disorders. *Behavioral Interventions, 25*, 157-168. doi: 10.1002/bin.300

Tiger, J. H., Hanley, G. P., & Bruzek, J. (2008). Functional communication training: A review and practical guide. *Behavior Analysis in Practice, 1*, 16-24.

Weitlauf, A. S., McPheeters, M. L., Peters, B., Sathe. N., Travis, R., Aiello, R., Williamson, E....& Warren, Z. (2014). Therapies for children with autism spectrum disorder: Behavioral interventions update. *Comparative Effectiveness Review* No. 137. (Prepared by the Vanderbilt Evidence-based Practice Center under Contract No. 290-2012-00009-I.) AHRQ Publication No. 14-EHC036-EF. Rockville, MD: Agency for Healthcare Research and Quality.

Wong, C., Odom, S. L., Hume, K. Cox, A. W., Fettig, A., Kucharczyk, S., Brock, M.E....& Schultz, T. R. (2015). Evidence-based practices for children, youth, and young adults with autism spectrum disorder. *Journal of Autism and Developmental Disorders, 45*(7), 1951-1966. doi: 10.1007/s10803-014-2351-z

Nurses and Mental Health Professionals: Collaborating to Meet the Healthcare Needs of Young Children with ASD

Constance E. McIntosh and Susan M. Wilczynski

Abstract

Preschool children with autism spectrum disorder (ASD) demonstrate behaviors and experience co-occurring conditions that can make learning basic health-related adaptive skills (e.g., learning hygiene) challenging. In addition, young children with ASD often have complex medical histories or require medications that can influence the appropriateness of specific assessments or interventions. Although healthcare services are sometimes offered in preschool settings, features associated with ASD can interfere with the effective delivery of healthcare within these settings. Registered Nurses (RNs) have a unique opportunity to share their understanding of medication administration, medical diagnosis, and disease processes with preschool staff, including mental health professionals. This paper provides an overview of healthcare issues commonly experienced by preschool children and how nurses can support preschool staff that have children with ASD in their care. Finally, strategies nurses can use to more effectively collaborate with mental health professionals and behavior specialists when addressing the healthcare and behavioral needs of preschool children with ASD and other disabilities are offered.

Key Words: ASD, nurses, mental health professionals, preschool, collaboration

Preschool staff serving typically developing young children are often able to address healthcare needs (e.g., medication administration, hand washing, clipping fingernails, etc.) and behavior (e.g., standing in line quietly, keeping hands off other preschoolers, playing quietly with other children, etc.) with minimal difficulty or without significant time commitment. For example, typically developing young children (ages 3 to 5) learn about proper hygiene (e.g., hand washing, brushing hair, covering nose when sneezing, etc.), receive simple first aid (e.g., bandage), and accept behavior correction from childcare workers and educational staff during the day. However, children with autism spectrum disorder (ASD) often demonstrate behavioral excesses (e.g., echolalia, stereotypic behavior, hypersensitivity, etc.) and have co-occurring conditions (e.g., anxiety, attention disorder, language delay, etc.) that make learning appropriate hygiene and social skills challenging.

ASD is a term used to describe a group of complex disorders of brain development, which can result in a variety of behaviors including impairments in social communication and repetitive (stereotypical) patterns of behavior and interests (American Psychological Association, 2013). Children with ASD often present with a unique combination of behaviors and symptoms that can make it difficult for preschool staff to provide even basic healthcare (Debbaudt, 2009). Challenging behaviors (e.g., kicking, hitting, tantrums, biting, punching, scratching; Hellings et al., 2005) can exacerbate the situation, while putting the preschool staff in harm's way (Debbaudt, 2009). Further complicating the issue, staff serving young children with ASD often report that they are inadequately trained and lack sufficient knowledge to care for supporting this population (McConkey & Bhlirgri, 2003). Young children with ASD who have significant language delays or who display severe behaviors may receive services through local school districts and Applied Behavior Analysis (ABA) clinics. However, many preschoolers with ASD are often placed in alternative settings where they can interact with typically developed peers (see Wilczynski et. al., this issue).

Registered Nurses (RNs) are in a unique position to collaborate with preschools that try to meet the healthcare and behavioral needs of children with ASD. RNs have expertise in disease symptoms, interventions, medications, and medical knowledge that can assist educational staff, behavior specialists, and mental health professionals. This paper provides an overview of healthcare issues found among preschool children, and describes how nurses can provide support to preschool workers who have children with ASD in their care. In addition, strategies that nurses can use to collaborate with mental health professionals and behavior specialists when addressing the healthcare and behavioral needs of preschoolers with ASD and other disabilities are highlighted.

Nurses and Children with Disabilities

Of the 53 million school children (5-17 years of age), approximately 2.8 million were reported to have a disability (US Census Bureau, 2010). Although exact statistics for young children are not available, estimates for the number of preschool children with disabilities can be extrapolated from data for older children. The National Center for Education Statistics (NCES, 2016) showed the prevalence of children receiving special education services has increased 14 percent from school years 1990 to 2004. For these school children, disabilities are categorized as specific learning disabilities, speech/language impairment, intellectual disability, development delay, emotional disturbance, and hearing impairment (NCES, 2016). The four remaining categories: other health impairments, ASD, multiple disabilities, and orthopedic impairments constitute 24% of the disabilities listed for school (NCES, 2016). Although these numbers reflect special education services in public school, it is reasonable to presume a similar proportion of young children, eventually attending public schools, would need similar assistance while at preschool. Given that the current prevalence rate of ASD falls at 1:68 children who are 8-years of age, a significant number of students with ASD are being served in the schools. Although it is still considered a low incidence disability, schools can now expect to provide services to children with ASD, including those in preschool.

Nurses can collaborate with other professionals to enhance the learning experiences of preschool children on the autism spectrum. Some children with ASD have significant gross and motor skill deficits that interfere with their capacity to learn and care for themselves (Ming, Brimacombe, & Wagner, 2009). Because of RNs' training in a wide range of health-related needs, they can help develop plans for self-skills such as dressing, brushing teeth, and hygiene. Cohen et al. (2011) highlighted the importance of interprofessional collaboration and resources for the CMC population. Medically fragile children, including children with special needs, chronic illnesses, and varying degrees of disabilities, require the benefits of an RN to provide safe and effective nursing interventions and to collaborate with professionals representing other disciplines (e.g., educational and mental health professionals).

Although the exact numbers of nursing interactions occurring with children with disabilities is unknown, the percentage of school children with disabilities mentioned above (24%) is consistent with the estimated percentage of patients with disabilities (25%) being admitted to the hospital daily. RNs' roles do not need to be restricted to traditional healthcare settings, however. A paucity of studies that explore healthcare services provided by nurses to preschool children with ASD or at ABA centers have been published. Given the increasing prevalence of ASD, the high percentage of co-occurring medical and psychiatric conditions found among children with ASD, and the increased focus on providing interprofessional services to children with ASD, it is surprising nurses are not seen as essential collaborators when developing accommodations in early childhood care and educational settings. The limited research that has been published in this area has primarily focused on school nurses and school children with ASD. For example, McIntosh (2013) found school nurses work with children with ASD by administering psychotropic, anti-seizure, anti-depressant, and a range of other medications. School nurses provide a variety of services including care for chronic health conditions, infection control measures, disease surveillance (Baisch, Lundeen, & Murphy, 2011), screenings, and disease prevention, as well as a focus on community/public health (Wold & Selekman, 2013).

When parents are asked to identify healthcare professionals they seek for their children, they do not list nurses as one of the healthcare professionals. Instead, parents are more likely to list speech/language pathologists, pediatricians, psychologists, and social workers among the needed healthcare providers (Cassidy et al., 2008). Although there are likely multiple reasons nurses were not listed as primary providers sought by parents (e.g., they associate nurses only with physicians), it points to the fact that adults responsible for the care of young children should be educated about the role nurses can play. Specifically, parents, preschool staff, behavior specialists, and child psychologists need education on how nurses can contribute to the development of healthcare-related interventions with children with ASD.

Addressing Common Health Issues of Young Children with ASD

Some childhood diseases (e.g., influenzas, conjunctivitis, Coxsackie virus, etc.) are commonly spread through viral and bacterial infections. These types of infections are spread through coughing, sneezing, and contact with an infected person (e.g., handshaking, toy sharing, and poor hygiene). To prevent the spread of viral and bacterial infections, there are a number of methods that can be used to teach preschoolers effective hand washing skills, including the five-step approach (wet hands, soap, lather front and back of hands, rinse, and dry with clean towel; Bowen et al., 2007) and adding rhymes/songs to make the steps fun (Rosen et al., 2009). Although teaching the aforementioned hand washing skills to typically developing children is relatively easy, helping children with ASD learn these skills, follow a hand washing routine, or overcome sensory issues related to hand washing can be difficult. Environmental factors can lead to sensory overload

(Murphy, Colwell, Pineda, & Bryan, 2006). Knowledge of sensory issues is necessary when communicating with children with ASD. RN's can provide specific verbal cues while assessing if the concepts are being understood. In addition, RNs can evaluate if the hand washing steps have been conducted properly.

Video modeling has been used to teach young children with ASD hand washing skills (Rosenberg, Schwartz, & Davis, 2010). Children with ASD were exposed to videos that were either commercially available or were custom made, using a child familiar to the preschooler as a model with the video (Rosenberg et al., 2010). The nine-step hand washing process (i.e., turn on water, wet hands, get soap, rub hands together, rinse hands, turn off the water, get a paper towel, dry hands, and throw away paper towel) in both sets of videos was used as the target steps and were 35-47 seconds in duration. One of three participants learned 80% of the target steps from the commercial video, while the other two participants responded better to the customized video (Rosenberg et al., 2010). Although limited research has been published related to studying effective methods for teaching preschool children with ASD hand washing skills, it is intuitive that RNs work directly with parents, preschool staff/teachers, and behavior specialists to help develop customized videos that are likely to produce the skills necessary. In fact, RNs can work collaboratively with parents and professionals to design and implement behavior programs with the goal of helping preschool children with ASD learn the nine-step hand washing process. Specifically, RNs can work with preschool staff and behavior specialists to establish a set hand washing routine, identify behaviors interfering with learning the routine, identify reinforcers (e.g., identifying edible reinforcers that are safe for a child with a developmental disability), and modify the routine, while maintaining the integrity of the hand washing routine. The RN can assist staff in developing and implementing a consistent hand washing routine, including developing a video demonstrating the required hand washing steps for preschoolers. In addition, the RN can assist in developing succinct commands and expectations, and label required objects if children are nonverbal. When on a predictable hand washing schedule, preschoolers with ASD are more likely to learn the hand washing process (Durand, Hieneman, Clarke, & Zona, 2009). As a result, young children with ASD are less likely to lose critical time from learning new skills because they will be absent from care and educational settings less frequently due to illness.

Despite the best efforts to reduce illness by teaching hand washing skills, young children with ASD will experience common diseases. The Centers for Disease Control and Prevention (CDC, 2016) report the average adult has 2-3 colds each year with children experiencing between 7-10 colds per year (Eccles, 2005). Viral and bacterial diseases have similar symptoms including fever, congestion, coughing, sore throat (post nasal drip), and watery eyes. Comfort measures (e.g., holding, rocking) that may work with typically developing children who have returned to preschool may be harder to use with children with ASD, especially preschoolers who experience sensory sensitivity. Rather, allowing children with ASD to rest in a "sensory room" or health room can assist in comforting them as they wait for a parent to arrive or until they start feeling better when they return to the preschool setting (Leekam et al., 2007). Keeping lights low, the room quiet (e.g., soft music), providing soft items (e.g., soft toys, big pillows, blankets), or a quiet space (e.g., a tent or large box to lay under) can be comforting to preschoolers with ASD. RNs may be more aware of the unique sensory needs of children with ASD and how to address these issues than the average preschool staff member.

Young children showing signs of sniffling, cough, and drainage would benefit from a set of vital signs (i.e., temperature, heart rate, respirations, and blood pressure) that can be easily provided by preschool staff. If within normal limits, comfort measures may be provided (e.g., tissues, water, and time away from demanding activities). Parents should be contacted if observation and vital signs indicate more than documentation of secretions (mucus, drainage). Preschool staff need to be prepared to take vital signs of children with ASD; otherwise, there will be an over-dependence on contacting parents to pick-up their children. Whereas the common cold is irritating to the average child, it can be deleterious to the preschooler with ASD. Time spent away from preschool environments that are rich with opportunities to learn new skills can mean that the skill gap between the child with ASD and their typically developing counterpart grows wider. Thus, educating staff on different techniques that can be used when taking the vitals of children with ASD is essential.

There are benefits to helping preschoolers with ASD to become familiar with the processes and procedures involved in taking vitals. Many children with ASD have significant communication limitations and cannot effectively tell others when they are unwell. Young children with ASD who can participate in the process of collecting these important health data are more likely to expeditiously receive treatment. RNs can play an essential role in the development of these skills. For example, RNs can work with staff, behavior specialists, and psychologists in developing a protocol that teaches preschool children with ASD to learn how to cooperate when vitals are taken. For example, a psychologist can incorporate the techniques during play therapy or a staff member can have a designated room within the center focused solely on RN and doctor visits. In addition, RNs can help develop visual schedules, which have also been successful for taking vital signs and other medical interventions (Chebuhar et al., 2012) with children with ASD. By becoming very familiar with the process of someone taking their vitals, preschoolers with ASD can avoid becoming fearful, agitated, or overly stimulated. Primarily, young children with ASD need to equate necessary medical procedures as nonthreatening, thus allowing medical professionals, preschool staff, as well as parents to provide timely and quality healthcare.

Children will be separated from their peers while parents come to pick them up when some childhood illnesses are highly contagious. For example, conjunctivitis (i.e., pink-eye) is highly contagious inflammation of the eyelid lining. Signs and symptoms include redness, yellowish-mucus, drainage, itchiness, and light sensitivity. Similarly, head lice are spread through sharing of hairbrushes, combs, blankets, and bedding. Preschool workers can identify these parasitic insects through frequent inspection of children's scalps. Because these types of illnesses require children to sit still during an inspection of the eye or scalp, early identification may be difficult for children with ASD. RNs are uniquely qualified to train staff on different methods that lead to accurate inspection of the eyes and scalp. For example, RNs are aware of the most likely location on the scalp where lice and nits can be found, reducing the time needed to search for lice.

Medication Administration within Preschool Settings

Children with ASD are diagnosed with medical and psychiatric comorbidities (e.g., mood disorders, aggression, depression, and self-injurious behaviors; Lecavalier, 2006). Research is unclear regarding the number of medications the average child with ASD takes to address these comorbid conditions; however, 46-50% of individuals with ASD are prescribed one or more medications for the management of comorbid conditions (Aman et al. 1995, 2003). Although many of these conditions are identified after the early childhood years, symptoms may be present during this period of life and off label (i.e., prescriptions that are not approved by the FDA; Good & Gelled, 2016) medications are often used to treat young children with ASD. Having an RN, an expert in medication administration, can help preschool staff members learn how to monitor side effects and develop interventions to assist in medication administration. It also is important for preschool staff to understand that some medication requires long-term maintenance support, compared to antibiotics where children complete their medication round. Finally, ASD medications prescribed during the preschool years to address comorbid conditions likely follow children from preschool to the school setting (Pringle, Colpe, Blumberg, Avila, & Kogan, 2012). Pringle et al. (2012) reported that over half of the school children (ages 6-17) are taking one, or a combination of two or more, medications (e.g., psychotropic, stimulant, anti-anxiety, mood-stabalizing, or anti-depressant) that are often prescribed for ASD.

There will be occasions when only a qualified health provider can administer medications to young children with ASD. McIntosh (2013) found school RNs' primary role when working with children with ASD was the administration of medication and medical treatment (e.g. seizure disorders, eating disorders). With seizure disorders emerging in the first five years of life (Myers et al., 2007), the RN can administer anticonvulsant medications while also monitoring side effects (e.g., dizziness, double or blurred vision, poor balance, headache, and stomach ache) of the medications. Monitoring side effects is especially important as medications used to treat seizures can often impact children's ability to learn (Sabers & Gram, 2000).

There are five main medication classifications of drugs (e.g., antihypertensive, antidepressants, antipsychotic, stimulants, and anticonvulsants) prescribed to children with ASD. Each classification of medication is used to treat specific symptoms, yet comes with side effects or common adverse reactions that must be monitored. Anticonvulsants have a variety of side effects (see aforementioned) but can also cause aggressive behavior and loss of appetite. Furthermore, some antipsychotic medications cause increased appetite and high prolactin levels (Masi et al., 2001). Monitoring the prolactin level is essential to avoid pituitary gland tumors. Nurses can establish such a monitoring schedule.

There are a wide variety of medications used to manage co-occurring conditions diagnosed along with an ASD. It is imperative RNs stay abreast of new treatment modalities and current medications, including side effects and drug interactions, prescribed to preschool children with ASD. By sharing this knowledge with preschool staff, behavior specialists, and psychologists who provide educational, behavioral, and psychological services, unnecessary and intrusive interventions may be avoided. For example, rather than having a behavior specialist complete a functional analysis of aggressive behavior and then generate a complex function-based intervention, the nurse can work with the family to recommend alternative medications when seizure-induced aggression is evident.

The National Health and Safety Performance Standards Guidelines for Early Care and Education Programs (Caring for Our Children, 2016) require preschool facilities to have written policies regarding the administration, acceptance, and storage/handling of medications because preschool workers are responsible for administering medication to children in their care (Sinkovits, Kelly, & Ernst, 2003). Policies only address the legal requirements of medication administration so staff are left on their own to problem solve how to administer medication when children refuse, spit out, have trouble swallowing, or choke when given medication. Behaviors (e.g., grabbing, crying, running away, slapping at the medication, biting, etc.) can quickly escalate when administering medication to children with ASD requiring the need for alternative approaches.

RNs, working closely with behavior specialists, can design visual schedules which include pictures, words, and dates/times that represent when medications should be taken. RNs can assist in determining whether medication can be mixed with certain foods and whether liquid or patch alternatives are available instead pills. However, when traditional alternatives have not been successful, behavioral methods to improve adherence with medication administration should be considered. For example, stimulus fading paired with positive reinforcement has been used to help a young boy with ASD learn to swallow medication (Schiff et al., 2011). The child experienced chronic ear infections and consistently refused oral medication. As a result, antibiotics had to be administered using a suppository (Schiff et al., 2011). Although the stimulus fading with reinforcement procedure was quite lengthy (i.e., a 54-step proce-dure), it resulted in a method that could be easily implemented by preschool staff.

Gastrointestinal (GI) Disorders and ASD

Children with ASD suffer from gastrointestinal (GI) disorders (e.g., chronic constipation, diarrhea, irritable bowel and inflamma-tory bowel) 3.5 times more often than typically developing children (CDC, 2016). The prevalence rates indicate GI disorders are among the most common medical conditions diagnosed among children with ASD. GI disorders can have far-reaching effects on preschoolers including pain leading to difficulty focusing and behavior issues.

RNs can write a nursing care plan for children with a GI dis-order that focuses on documenting the pattern of diarrhea or constipation that can be followed by preschool staff. Recording the toileting frequency shows patterns of characteristics, amount, and precipitating factors of the stool. Assessing the GI track through auscultation, palpation, and percussion, provides the nurse with a complete picture of what is happening within children's GI track (Vera, 2013). By working together, nurses and behavior specialists can implement interventions such as a regular toileting schedule. RNs can work with parents and staff in evaluating nutritional intake (e.g., too little or too much fiber) and be the liaison with the primary physician to identify medications needed to assist in addressing the disorder. Working with a behavior specialist, nurses can identify methods for providing comfort to preschoolers, such as eliminating certain smells that irritate the condition, tummy rubs, and frequent rests. Developing a toileting routine may prevent painful gas and bloating, allowing for a better preschool and classroom experience.

General Role of Nurses During the Preschool Years

Preschools rarely employ a full-time RN on staff. Cost restric-tions should not negate the importance the RN can play in these settings, however. The RN can work with mental health profession-als in providing workshops, sharing medication knowledge (e.g., usage, side effects of medications), and determining when to refer to a nurse practitioner or physician. The RN can provide guidance, interventions, and education in working with preschoolers with ASD. Costs to employ an RN on a full time basis is a factor that preschools have to consider. Yet, hiring an RN on a consultation basis or an as-needed basis is a viable solution that bridges the need and the financial consideration. At a minimum, RNs can provide workshops on what young children with ASD can expect when visiting a hospital or healthcare clinic. Role-playing a trip to the physician's office may help alleviate anxiety. A field trip to a clinic, emergency department, or hospital may help introduce unfamiliar surroundings to preschoolers with ASD.

Preschool settings often reported the concerns of parents and parents who have children diagnosed with ASD who often find it difficult to find helpful, professional support (Cassidy et al., 2008). Because RNs are familiar with healthcare professionals and consistently plan for the next level of care, including community care, it makes sense that a nurse can make the necessary resource connections including speech/language therapists, pediatricians, psychologists, social workers, and respite care.

An interprofessional approach is taken when patients are admitted to the hospital. The same type of approach should be taken serving preschoolers with ASD in commonly accessed early childhood settings. RNs and mental health professionals can support each other as they each focus on the well-being of the individual including, physical, mental, emotional, and the social aspects of the child. RNs can educate health professionals, behavior specialists, and early childhood staff on different aspects of ASD comorbidities, including allergies, seizures, gastrointestinal problems, plus the respiratory and ear infections that often accompany children with ASD. RNs can translate medical diagnoses, diseases, and medical records to other healthcare professionals.

Explaining medical, disease, medication, and intervention information about children's diagnoses to therapists (e.g., speech/language, physical, occupational, behavioral) is an important role of the nurse. The RN can share how the overall medical picture can influence learning, the educational experience, and other team interventions. Explaining routine monitoring parameters for continued medication use is essential including routine lab draws, blood draws, liver functions, height, weight, and vital signs.

RNs can identify medication side effects, adverse reactions, and interactions. Translating drug information for professionals representing different disciplines is another area where nurses are uniquely able to contribute to the welfare of young children with ASD. A comprehensive home medical model that includes coordinated care between professionals and family best meets the needs of preschoolers with ASD. Providing this kind of patient-centered care can be extended to early childhood settings to avoid the risk of medical concerns falling through the cracks. Medical information and treatment modalities can get lost when mental health professionals are focused on the psychological aspect of ASD and preschool teachers are focused on the educational piece. The RN can effectively explain how the medical conditions affect the child with ASD and facilitate comprehensive approaches to treatment.

The RN can help in coordinating care with the home. Keeping the parents informed about the daily activities of children can prove beneficial. For example, alerting parents about head lice inspections before the event so the parents can begin preparing the child. A nurse can provide necessary information to family members when young children with ASD need to seek medical attention. For example, if given the choice between a physician clinic and an emergency department (ED), parents should select the physician clinic because EDs are not ideal for treating preschoolers with ASD due to the noise distractions, various healthcare providers in one visit, competing demands (Zwaigenbaum et al., 2016), and potential wait times. Conversely, physician clinics have the same personnel, are quieter, schedule appointments, and have a slower paced environment.

There are significant opportunities for an RN to be involved when a preschool child is transitioning into the school system. Schools nurses coordinate the care of students through assessment, diagnosis, outcome identification, planning, and evaluations (National Association for School Nurses, 2016). For an easier transition from preschool to school, the RN can easily share information about children's routines with the school nurse. In addition, the RN can share the schedule and routine of medication administration, and ways to successfully decrease stimulation. Sharing information with the school nurse on behavioral interventions (e.g., current reward systems) and how to successfully transition from preschool to school should also be discussed. In order for the interprofessional team to be complete, an RN should be included when designing and implementing special education services. RNs' understanding of common medical conditions (i.e., depression, ADHD, seizures, etc.) found to co-occur with ASD can assist in the development of an evaluation plan and when developing academic accommodations (McIntosh & Thomas, 2015).

Summary

RNs, preschool staff, and mental health professionals have a common goal of providing care to young children, while also complementing each unique role. When working with preschoolers with ASD, nurses have a broad range of skill sets (i.e. communication, critical thinking, and medical knowledge) that can lead to a better clinical and educational experience. Medications are an important aspect of the treatment plan. However, for young children with ASD, the medication maintenance (i.e., the side effects, adverse effects, and taking the medication) can be challenging. Working with the mental health professionals can establish a successful medication schedule. Assisting with smooth transitions from home to preschool and, eventually, from preschool to school, is another way nurses can collaborate. Formal communication between the RN who is working with a preschool team and school nurse can contribute to a reward system, medication administration, and healthcare picture (i.e., behavior issues, medical comorbidities) that results in a successful transition for young children with ASD.

Authors Note

Correspondence concerning this article should be addressed to Constance E. McIntosh, RN, Ed.D.; cemcintosh@bsu.edu.

References

Aman, M.G., Van Bourgondien, M.E., Worlford, P. L., & Sarphare, G. (1995). Psychotropic and anticonvulsant drugs in subjects with Autism: Prevalence and patterns of use. *Journal of American Academy Child Adolescent Psychiatry, 34*(12), 1672-1681.

Aman, M., Lam, K, & Collier-Crespin, A. (2003). Prevalence and patterns of use of psychoactive medications among individuals with Autism in the Autism Society of Ohio. *Journal of Autism and Development Disorders, 33*(5), 527-534. doi: 10.1023/A:1025883612879

American Psychological Association. (2013). *Diagnostic and statistical manual of mental disorders* (5th ed.). Arlington, VA: American Psychiatric Publishing.

Baisch, M. J., Lundeen, S.P., & Murphy, M.K. (2011). Evidence-based research on the value of school nurses in an urban school system. *The Journal of School Health, 81*(2), 74-80. doi:10.1111/j.1746-1561/2010.00563.x

Bowen, A., Ma, H., Ou, J., Billhimer, W., Long, T., Mintz, E.,...& Luby, S. (2007). A cluster-randomized controlled trial evaluating the effect of a hand washing-promotion program in Chinese primary schools. *The American Society of Tropical Medicine and Hygiene. 76*(6), 1166-1173.

Caring for Our Children (2016). National Health and Safety Performance Standards Guidelines for Early Care and Education Programs. Retrieved on 09/07/2016. http://cfoc.nrckids.org/StandardView/9.2.3.9.

Cassidy, A., McConkey, R., Truesdale-Kennedy, M., & Slevin, E. (2008). Preschoolers with Autism Spectrum Disorders: The impact of families and the supports available to them. *Early Child Development and Care. 178*(2), 115-128.

Centers for Disease Control and Prevention (CDC, 2016). Concurrent medical conditions and health care use and needs among children with learning and behavioral developmental disabilities. National Health Interview Survey, 2006-2010. Retrieved on 09/07/2016 http://www.ncbi.nlm.nih.gov/pubmed/22119694.

Centers for Disease Control and Prevention (CDC, 2016). Common colds: protect yourself and others. Retrieved on 08/30/2016 http://www.cdc.gov/features/rhinoviruses/.

Chebuhar, A. McCarthy, A., & Bosch, J. (2012). Using picture schedules in medical settings for patients with Autism Spectrum Disorder. *Journal of Pediatric Nursing. 28*(2), 125-134.

Cohen, E., Kuo, D., Agrawal, R., Berry, J., Bhagat, S., Simon, T., & Srivastava, R. (2011). Children with medical complexity: An emerging population for clinical and research initiatives. *Pediatrics, 127*(3), 529-538.

Debbaudt, D. (2009). Patients with Autism and other high risks: A growing challenge for healthcare security. *Journal of Healthcare Protection Management, 25*(1), 14-26.

Durand, V., Hieneman, M., Clarke, S., & Zona, M. (2009). Optimistic parenting: Hope and help for parents with challenging children. *Handbook of Positive Behavior Support, 2.* 233-236. NY: Springer.

Eccles, R. (2005). Understanding the symptoms of the common cold and influenza. *Lancet Infection Diseases. 5*(11), 718-725.

Good, C. B., & Gelled, W. F. (2016). Off-label drug use and adverse drug events: Turning up the heat on off-label prescribing. *JAMA Internal Medicine, 176*(1), 63-64.

Hellings, J., Nickel, E., Weckbaurgh, M., McCarter, K., Mosier, M., & Schroeder, S. (2005). The overt aggression scale on outpatient youth with autistic disorder: Preliminary findings. *Journal of Neuropsychiatry Clinical Neuroscience, 17*(1). 29-35.

Lecavalier, L. (2006). Behavioral and emotional problems in young people with pervasive developmental disorders: Relative prevalence, effects of subject characteristics, and empirical classification. *Journal of Autism and Developmental Disorders, 36*(8), 1101-1114. doi: 10.1007/s10803-006-0147-5

Leekam, S., Libby, S., Wing, L., & Gould, J. (2007). Describing the sensory abnormalities of children and adults with autism. *Journal of Autism & Developmental Disorders, 31*(5), 894-910.

Masi, G., Cosenza, A., Mucci, M., & Brovedani, P. (2003). A 3-year naturalistic study of 53 preschool children with pervasive developmental disorders treated with Risperidone. *Journal of Clinical Psychiatry, 64*(9), 1039-1047.

McConkey, R., & Bhlirgri, S. (2003). Children with Autism attending preschool facilities: The experiences and perceptions of staff. *Early Child Development and Care. 172*, 443-452.

McIntosh, C. (2013). A national survey of school nurses and Autism Spectrum Disorders (ASD). www.cardinalscholar.bsu.edu

McIntosh, C. E., & Thomas, C. M. (2015). Utilization of school nurses during the evaluation and identification of children with Autism Spectrum Disorders. *Psychology in the Schools. 52*(7), 648-657.

Ming, X., Brimacombe, M., & Wagner, G. (2009). Prevalence of motor impairment in Autism Spectrum Disorder. *Brain & Development. 29*(9). 265-570.

Murphy, P., Colwell, C., Pineda, G., & Bryan, T. (2006). Breaking down barriers: How EMS providers can communicate with Autistic patients. *EMS World.* http://www.emsworld.com/article/online

Myers, S. M., Johnson, C. P., & The American Academy of Pediatrics Council of Children with Disabilities (AAPCCD; 2007). Management of children with autism spectrum disorders. *Pediatrics, 120*(5), 1162-1182.

National Association for School Nurses. (2016). Framework for 21st century school nursing practice. *NASN School Nurse, 31*(1), 45-53. doi: 10.1177/1942602x15618644

National Center for Education Statistics. (2016). Children and youth with disabilities. Retrieved on 09/07/2016. http://nces.ed.gov/programs/coe/indicator_cgg.asp

Pringle, B. A., Colpe, L. J., Blumberg, S. J., Avila, R. M., Kogan, M. D. (2012). Diagnostic history and treatment of school-aged children with Autism Spectrum Disorder and Special Health Care Needs. *National Center for Health Statistics (NCHS): Data Brief* (97).

Rosen, L., Zucker, D., Brody, D., Engelhard, D., & Manor, O. (2009). The effect of a hand washing intervention on preschool educator beliefs, attitudes, knowledge and self-efficacy. *Health Education Research. 24*(4), 686-698.

Rosenberg, N. E., Schwartz, I. S., & Davis, C. A. (2010). Evaluating the utility of commercial videotapes for teaching hand washing to children with autism. *Education and Treatment of Children, 33*(3), 443-455.

Sabers, A., & Gram, L. (2000). Newer anticonvulsants. *Drugs. 60*(1), 23-33.

Schiff, A., Tarbox, J., Lanagan, T., & Farag, P. (2011). Establishing compliance with liquid medication administration in a child with Autism. *Journal of Applied Behavior Analysis. 44*(2), 381-385.

Sinkovits, H. S., Kelly, M. W., & Ernst, M. E. (2003). Medication administration in day care centers for children. *Journal of American Pharmacists Association.* *43*(3), 379-382.

United States Census Bureau (2010). United States Department of Commerce: Economics and Statistics Administration. Retrieved on 09/07/2016. https://www.census.gov/prod/2011pubs/acsbr10-12.pdf

Vera, M. (2013). Nurselabs: For all your nurses needs: Seven inflammatory bowel disease (IBD) nursing care plans. Retrieved on 09/07/2016. http://nurseslabs.com/7-inflammatory-bowel-disease-nursing-care-plans/

Wilczynski, S. M., Trammel, B., Caugherty, N., Shellabarger, K., McIntosh, C., & Kaake, A. (current issue). *Perspectives in Early Childhood Psychology and Education.*

Wold, S. & Selekman, J. (2013). *School Nursing: A Comprehensive Text* (2nd ed.), 79-108. Philadelphia, PA: F. A. Davis & Company.

Zwaigenbaum, L., Nicholas, D., Muskat, B., Kilmer, C., Newton, A., Craig, W., & Sharon, R. (2016). Perspectives of health care providers regarding emergency department care of children and youth with Autism Spectrum Disorder. *Journal of Autism and Developmental Disorders, 46*(5), 1725-1736.

Evidence-Based Practice, Culture, and Young Children with Autism Spectrum Disorder

Susan M. Wilczynski, Amanda Henderson, Nicholas R. Harris, Sonia D. Kosmala, and Jessica Bostic

Abstract

Evidence-based practice (EBP) involves using professional judgment to integrate the best available evidence with a client's values and preferences to make decisions that help the client make meaningful progress. To effectively employ evidence-based practice as a decision-making model, early childhood practitioners need to understand the range of ways issues of culture can influence decisions to select, retain, adapt, or reject an intervention. There is a paucity of research on cultural variables and autism treatment during early childhood; therefore, the authors briefly reviewed the conceptualization of culture as it broadly relates to the evidence-based practice literature. We examine ways in which culture may be relevant to the scientific literature involving young children with ASD and to the values and preferences of clients. Strategies for incorporating preferences of young children with ASD are offered. In addition, the role parent preferences and values have in the identification of appropriate treatments for young children with ASD is described, with special consideration given to the way cultural membership can influence these perspectives. Finally, recommendations for practitioners are made to enhance the cultural sensitivity of their professional judgment when serving young children with ASD.

Key words: diversity, culture, autism spectrum disorder, early childhood, evidence-based practice

Evidence-based practice (EBP) is a decision-making model that guides practitioners in selecting and retaining effective interventions (Slocum, Detrich, Wilczynski, Spencer, Lewis, & Wolfe, 2014). EBP requires the use of sound professional judgment to integrate the best available evidence with the values and preferences of clients (Sackett and colleagues, circa 1990). The EBP decision-making model should result in the selection of the "right" treatment for a given client (Slocum et al., 2014), with an understanding that the best treatment may be dependent on a range of contextual factors.

The EBP decision-making model can be applied to all populations. However, because autism spectrum disorder (ASD) is one the fastest growing developmental disorders, practitioners must understand how to apply the EBP model to this population. The gap between individuals diagnosed with ASD and their typically developing peers is smallest at early ages and, therefore, early intervention can maintain a smaller gap (Volkmar, Chawarska, & Klin, 2005) or close the gap altogether (Howard, Stanislaw, Green, Sparkman, & Cohen, 2014). Selecting and implementing the "right" treatment is critical in meeting this goal.

Culture is a variable that should be considered when deliberating between treatment options. For the purposes of this article, culture is defined as membership in groups on the basis of race, ethnicity, sex, socioeconomic status, age, or other human attributes that can influence the social norms or expectations of the group. Although some experts argue that the greatest good can be accomplished for the vast majority of people when universal treatments are identified (LaRoche, Davis, & D'Angelo, 2014), this perspective has been described as culturally insensitive. The EBP decision-making model allows practitioners to consider the impact of culture in each essential component: evidence, preferences/values, and professional judgment. However, there is a dearth of literature describing how this applies to early childhood. This article begins with a brief review of the characteristics and associated features of ASD. Next, the components of EBP are reviewed so that practitioners can understand the value of different forms of evidence and client values/preferences. Culture is then examined in relation to the components of EBP as it applies to the ASD population, with an emphasis on young children (under six years of age). Finally, strategies practitioners can use to increase the cultural sensitivity of their professional judgment are reviewed.

Autism Spectrum Disorder

ASD is a developmental disorder that has been diagnosed equally across racial, ethnic, and economic groups (Tincani, Travers, & Boutot, 2009). The Centers for Disease Control and Prevention (CDC; 2016) estimates that 1 in 68 children in the United States have been diagnosed with ASD. Male prevalence (1 in 42) is significantly higher than female prevalence (1 in 189). The key characteristics of ASD are deficits in social-communication and excesses in fixated interests, repetitive movements, or rigid adherence to routines (American Psychiatric Association [APA], 2013; Matson, Kozlowski, Hattier, Horovitz, & Sipes, 2012). Communication occurs in the form of spoken language, sign language, gestures, or alternative communication devices (Heath, Ganz, Parker, Burke, & Ninci, 2015). Irrespective of the form taken, communication is an instrument for socially interacting with others in meaningful ways. The inability to develop, maintain, and understand relationships is a key characteristic of ASD (APA, 2013). Although many young children with ASD engage in some degree of play, social participation, and social interaction (McGee, Feldman, & Morrier (1997), young children with ASD spend less time in close proximity to other children, receive fewer bids for social interaction from peers, produce fewer verbalizations, and engage in more atypical behavior when compared to typically developing children (McConnell, 2002).

The restricted and repetitive behaviors that characterize ASD include stereotyped or repetitive motor movements (e.g. lining up toys), insistence on sameness (e.g. difficulty with transitions), or highly restricted or fixated interests (e.g., preoccupation with unusual objects); (Diagnostic and Statistical Manual; APA, 2013), At one time, severe problems with restricted and repetitive behaviors were thought to be somewhat rare in preschoolers or toddlers with ASD (Charman & Baird, 2002; Stone, Lee, & Weis, 1999; Ventola et al.,2006). However, recent studies have confirmed what parents have known all along, these maladaptive behaviors are clearly present in many infants, toddlers, and preschoolers who are later diagnosed with ASD (Richler, Bishop, Kleinke & Lord, 2007; Watson, Baranek, Crais, Reznick, Dykstra, & Perryman, 2007).

Evidence-Based Practice

Best Available Evidence

Ideally, many well-controlled studies show a treatment works and that treatment is deemed "effective." However, the label "evidence-based" has become ubiquitous and, as a result, its meaning has been weakened. Practitioners must consider the source, methodology, and scholarship involved in identifying effective treatment to critically evaluate the quality of the review (Wilczynski, 2012). There are multiple strategies for evaluating the treatment literature such as systematic reviews, alternate reviews, and client history (Slocum et al., 2012).

Systematic reviews. Systematic reviews identify effective treatments by evaluating the quality, quantity, and consistency of research outcomes (Moher, Liberati, Tetzlaff, & Altman, 2009; Slocum et al., 2012). Systematic reviews are the least biased source of evidence and are therefore considered the best source of evidence (Slocum et al., 2012). The prior opinions of the scholars completing a systematic review do not pre-determine the outcomes or influence which studies will be included in the analysis.

Although systematic reviews are considered the "best," they are not a perfect source of evidence. There are no universal standards for conducting systematic reviews so a review of the same literature (e.g., young children with ASD) can result in different outcomes. For example, the National Standards Project 2.0 (National Autism Center [NAC], 2015) identified functional communication training (FCT) as having only "emerging" evidence of effectiveness while the Evidence-Based Practice for Children Youth, and Young Adults with Autism Spectrum Disorder Report (Wong et al., 2015) described FCT as effective. The difference in outcomes results from using slightly different methodologies. Despite the fact that these differences emerge, the outcomes tend to overlap considerably because similar variables are evaluated in systematic reviews. The quality of the research design and dependent measure, as well as evidence of treatment fidelity, are typically included in these reviews, but additional variables may be considered (e.g., participant ascertainment, generality; Wilczynski, 2012). Practitioners should understand the criteria scientists adopt whenever they use the results of a systematic review so they can draw their own conclusions about the credibility of the document.

Practitioners should evaluate systematic reviews in terms of how well the results apply to the young child with ASD (client) they are serving. For example, research might be conducted in a highly controlled laboratory setting in which the interventionist (i.e., person implementing the treatment) is solely focused on treatment fidelity. However, treatments are likely to be applied in the toddler's or preschooler's home, school, or community by parents or teachers who have many competing demands on their time. Treatment effectiveness is often lower when a treatment is transported into real-world settings (Weisz, Jensen-Doss, & Hawley, 2006) and differences in context (e.g., setting and interventionist) can contribute to these poorer outcomes.

Cultural membership may also represent a source of discrepancy between research and practice. Clients may be dissimilar to research participants based on features of age, diagnosis, developmental level, ethnicity, socioeconomic status, and sex. The extent to which the results apply for a given client may be dependent on these characteristics or cultural memberships. For example, the

National Standards Report (NAC, 2009) reviewed 22 studies on Early Intensive Behavioral Intervention (EIBI; or comprehensive behavioral treatment for young children). This comprehensive treatment involves a 1:1 therapist-to-child ratio (particularly early in treatment) with behavioral interventions (e.g., discrete trial instruction) being delivered for 20-40 hours per week for up to four years (Peters-Scheffer, Didden, Korzilius, & Sturney, 2011; Reichow, Barton, Boyd, & Hume, 2012). We examined the race and sex of participants described in the studies included in the National Standards Report (NAC, 2009). Only 20% of these studies identified the race of the participants. Of the 147 participants in these studies for whom race was reported, 63% were White, 5% Black, 10% Asian Americans, and 13% Hispanic. This sample does not accurately reflect the representation of these groups based on population statistics in the United States. Sex of participants, which was almost always identified in the studies, was also examined across these 22 studies. Representation of both sexes was not equal in these studies, but this is not surprising given the disproportionate rate of ASD among males as compared to females (CDC; 2016). However, although representation is proportional to prevalence across the sexes, under-representation of young females in treatment research is still problematic for the practitioner trying to determine whether or not the outcomes reported in research apply to the client being served.

Narrative reviews. There are two types of narrative reviews. A consensus review is when a group of experts draw from their vast knowledge about research outcomes and endorse treatments that they agree have been effective in the literature. A critical review is often completed by a researcher (or team of researchers) who has a special interest in a given topic. Consensus and critical reviews provide less believable evidence because bias and/or politics are more likely to influence whether or not a treatment is considered effective (Slocum et al., 2012). However, narrative reviews may match the specifics of a given case better than a systematic review so they should not be ignored despite their limitations.

Narrative reviews are more prone to bias than systematic reviews so issues of diversity may be more likely to impact interpretation of outcomes. For example, the team of experts convened to render their expert opinions about the effectiveness of a given treatment may have spent their careers trying to show a given treatments works. They will be subject to confirmation bias (Wason, 1960) and may ignore the limitations of the research. Research they identify as having the highest quality of scientific evidence may poorly represent preschool girls or Black toddlers. When relying on either systematic or narrative reviews, practitioners must recognize that the quality of evidence may be weaker for some clients due to issues of diversity.

Scant information is available about parental income or educational attainment and participation in Early Intensive Behavioral Intervention; therefore, firm conclusions about socioeconomic status cannot be made. However, literature representing older populations shows that more highly educated and higher income households are over-represented in research (Robert & House, 1996). It is likely that young children with ASD coming from lower income households headed by parents with lower levels of educational attainment are not as well represented in the autism treatment literature. Thus, the extent to which the level of treatment effectiveness reported in the literature applies equally to this population is unknown.

Client history. Client history can be a valuable source of information about treatment effectiveness, but it is not necessarily without bias with respect to cultural membership. Treatment fidelity refers to the extent to which an intervention is accurately implemented. A high degree of treatment fidelity cannot be achieved unless the materials needed for therapy are available and the person implementing the intervention has been adequately trained. Client history could suggest a treatment was not effective but these data reflect poor treatment fidelity more than the client's capacity to respond to the intervention. Thus, socioeconomic status may impact the credibility of evidence drawn from client history. That is, client history may not be a good predictor of outcomes if resources could now be directed toward these dimensions (i.e., materials and training). Still, practitioners should not ignore this important form of evidence because it predicts the likelihood the treatment will be effective under similar conditions.

Client Values and Preference

Although research should guide the selection of treatments, practitioners using the evidence-based practice model also give due consideration to the values and preferences of clients (Guyatt et al., 1992; Slocum et al., 2014). As a result of their age and developmental level, young children with ASD are not directly involved in the selection of treatments. However, decisions about treatment appropriateness occurs at two points and there are opportunities for incorporating the preferences of young children with disabilities at both points. First, a treatment is initially selected to answer a practical question (Spencer, Detrich, & Slocum, 2012). For example, "How can we decrease Jeremiah's hand flapping?" or "How can we increase Tammy's appropriate social interactions with peers?" Treatments that incorporate child preference should be given a higher priority. For example, young children with ASD can participate in preference assessments and the materials identified in a preference assessment can be used in a reinforcement-based intervention. Preference assessments have been effectively conducted with preschool-aged children (Jones, Dozier, & Neidert, 2014; Layer, Hanley, Heal, & Tiger, 2008). Although limited research has been conducted with infants and toddlers, research involving individuals with severe cognitive impairments have offered procedural variants that may be highly appropriate for infants or toddlers who are not capable of selecting from an array of items (Rush, Mortenson, & Birch, 2010). Young children can also express preference when offered choices. In fact, treatment effectiveness has increased among 3, 4, and 5-year old children with ASD when choice was incorporated into treatments (Toussaint, Kodak, & Vladescu, 2016). Similarly, treatments that increase access to preferred materials (e.g., environmental enrichment, non-contingent reinforcement) can incorporate even the youngest child's interests. These treatments will not always answer the practical question, but when they do, they should be given a higher priority in the treatment selection process. There are no data regarding young children, but there are cultural differences for preference regarding different treatments with older children (Elliott, Turco, Evans, & Gresham, 1984). By incorporating unique preferences into treatment and offering choices that are culturally sensitive, evidence-based practitioners can address culturally influenced preferences for treatments.

Second, after the treatment has been implemented, the next evidence-based practice decision involves determining if the intervention should be retained, adapted, or rejected. Client preference can easily be assessed at this point by examining a young child's negative or positive enthusiasm and/or affect when treatment is delivered. Clients who cry, push materials away, or express distress do not prefer a treatment (Koegel, Werner, Vismara, & Koegel, 2005). An effective treatment that is associated with negative enthusiasm and affect might reasonably be adapted or rejected if a viable alternative is feasible. However, evaluation of emotional expression may be influenced by cultural membership (Zebrowitz, Kikuchi, & Fellous, 2010). Thus, evidence-based practitioners must ensure that they are collecting objective data that have strong inter-observer agreement. Ideally, practitioners receive training on data collection for affect with members of different races and inter-observer agreement is high.

Parents' values and preferences should be fully integrated into the decision-making process as treatments are selected, retained, adapted, or rejected. Practitioners are often trained in scientific methods so it is easy to place inordinate emphasis on the results of a systematic review, without giving due consideration to the limitations of this source of evidence. Practitioners risk placing their own cultural beliefs and expectations on a family (Green, Pituch, Itchon, Choi, O'Reilly, & Sigafoos, 2006) and recommend interventions that either do not align with the family's belief systems or are not feasible for the family due to resource constraint or limited environmental supports. Practitioners may also inadvertently engage in microaggressions (Constantine, 2007) when they discount the importance of parent's beliefs. Treatment goals and interventions should only be selected after practitioners understand and incorporate the cultural views and practices of the family (Hwang, 2006). Practitioners must avoid either turning parents away from services altogether by advocating only one alternative or leaving parents with the feeling they are unable to manage the care required for their child (Dyches, Wilder, Sudweeks, Obiakor, & Algozzine, 2004).

Treatment acceptability (i.e., the extent to which an intervention is palatable) should be evaluated as an important source of information in the EBP decision-making process. Treatment acceptability is typically assessed through a questionnaire format, with parents rating a treatment based on tolerability, fairness, and/or expected effectiveness. Limited data are available about the appropriateness of treatment acceptability questionnaires for diverse populations. For example, the 15-item Treatment Evaluation Inventory (TEI), which is one of the most valid tools for measuring stakeholders' views about acceptability, may be too verbally loaded for those parents who lack adequate literacy skills (Finn & Sladeczek, 2001). Differences in treatment acceptability may emerge based on the sex of the person completing the questionnaire. Mothers and fathers have different views about treatment acceptability. Mothers rate treatments as more acceptable than fathers when their children demonstrate problem behavior (Miller & Kelley, 1992), but fathers find medical treatments as more acceptable (Dahl, Tervo, & Symons, 2007; Miller & Kelley, 1992). When alternate intervention options are being considered for young children with ASD, evidence-based practitioners should assess treatment acceptability for all parents so that all parent's views are incorporated into treatment selection. Perceived support (e.g., tangible and emotional assistance) offered by immediate and extended family members is associated with higher treatment acceptability (Pemberton & Borrego, 2005). However, family support cannot be assumed. Cross-generational coalitions can reduce the likelihood a given treatment will be effective (Powers, 1991). Practitioners should carefully assess any family dysfunctionality and consider how this may impact treatment selection, retention, adaption, or rejection. Strategies for enhancing familial support should be examined (e.g., parents can reach out to family members who have appeared neutral).

Parental views about feasibility should also influence the treatment selection process. Any number of factors related to resource constraint and/or environmental supports can influence the viability of a given treatment. For example, EIBI is cost prohibitive for many families (Chasson, Harris, & Neely, 2007) particularly because mothers of children with ASD earn considerably less than mothers of children with other health challenges (35% less) and mothers whose children do not experience health limitations (56% less; Cidav, Marcus, & Madell, 2012). Parental views about feasibility are not restricted to financial resources. Parents have successfully implemented a range of effective interventions, such as EIBI (Strauss, Vicari, Valeri, D'Elia, Arimia, & Fava, 2012) and Pivotal Response Training (Gengouxet al., 2015). Treatments are more likely to result in improvements when parents actively implement behavioral interventions (Dunlap, Newton, Fox, Benito, & Vaughn, 2001). Yet, it may not be viable for all parents to implement these interventions and their views about feasibility may be connected to cultural membership. For example, parents may be unable to commit the time required to fully participate in extensive and on going training due to non-work commitments (e.g., the needs of their other children, or active participation in a religious community). In addition, socioeconomic status and level of parental education can impact a parent's understanding of, interest in, and willingness to implement interventions (Poslawsky, Naber, Van Daalen, & Engeland, 2014; Tincani et al., 2009).

The cultural group to which a parent belongs often holds expectations that influence parental levels of comfort with providing treatment to their children (Dyches et al., 2004). For example, discrete trial training, an important component of EIBI, typically begins with delivering a command to the young child with ASD and ends with contingent delivery of reinforcement (Smith, 2001). Women are often weaker at delivering directives to their children (Leaper, Anderson, & Sanders, 1998) and can experience distress resulting from the conflict between the cultural expectation of being nurturing and adopting the most effective strategy for delivering commands. In addition, withholding attention, praise, or "fun" activities when their child does not perform a task correctly can create significant discomfort. Finally, members of their group (e.g., women with strong views of mothers as nurturers) may make critical comments to a parent. When these members of a cultural group are the primary source of support for a parent, it is not surprising that accurate implementation of an intervention may be compromised. Ideally, treatments that are consistent with cultural views are selected. Practitioners can also help parents to resolve cultural conflict when challenges are anticipated (e.g., explain strategies for discussing with members of the cultural group how nurturing a child with ASD may look different).

Combining all Sources of Information

EBP begins with a practical question focusing on how a problem behavior or the lack of a skill interferes with the success at home, school, or in the community. Practitioners must use their professional judgment to examine multiple forms of evidence that can answer that practical question. Treatments that have higher quality evidence from multiple sources should be given higher priority for all young children, irrespective of the cultural groups in which they are members. However, practitioners must take care to question these sources of evidence. Greater skepticism must be brought to bear whenever the evidence drawn from research does not reflect the characteristics, the context, or cultural membership of the client.

Parent and child preferences should be incorporated into decision-making process. For example, some parents may prefer incidental teaching to capitalize on naturally occurring learning opportunities that easily fit into routine household activities. Other parents may prefer treatments that are delivered under more structured conditions so they might prefer discrete trial instruction. Both of these treatments can be effective with young children with ASD so parent input should drive the decision-making process. Practitioners should facilitate realistic discussions about treatment acceptability, feasibility, and parents' values. Lastly, practitioners should obtain ongoing training to become multiculturally competent. Therapeutic outcomes can be compromised if a treatment is prematurely terminated due to cultural insensitivity.

Recommendations

The EBP decision-making model allows the practitioner to select and adapt treatments to produce positive outcomes for all clients. The following recommendations to practitioners are made regarding EBP and culture. Due to the paucity of evidence in this area, these suggestions are offered broadly (i.e., they are not specific to young children).

1. Examine multiple sources and consider the relevance of evidence for the current client. Because all forms of evidence will not perfectly match the current client, the practitioners own cultural biases may impact their weighting for different forms of evidence. Practitioners should assess the their own biases when evaluating different forms of evidence.

2. The National Standards Project 2.0 and the Evidence-Based Practices for Children, Youth, and Young Adults with Autism

Spectrum Disorders Report (Wong et al., 2015) provide information about treatment effectiveness for young children with ASD. These are only two of the systematic reviews that shed light on treatment for young children with ASD.

3.   Client values and preferences should be assessed frequently throughout the early childhood years. Perceptions about treatment acceptability often alter over time and parents may be more willing to share concerns about barriers to implementation when a relationship with the service provider continues over time.

4.   Environmental supports or resource constraints may change over time so repeated evaluation of these variables is needed to maintain a good contextual fit. A family may change socioeconomic status or new members of a family may impact familial support in a way that alters the appropriateness of a given treatment.

5.   Parental participation in the treatment selection, retention, adaptation, or rejection process is critical. Some parents may not have strong advocacy skills, however (Powers, 1991). Practitioners can help parents develop advocacy skills so that treatments that are acceptable and feasible will be implemented with fidelity.

6.   Parents are more likely to be resilient in the face of distress and adversity when they have a strong social network. Practitioners can encourage parents to develop and maintain social networks, including autism support groups, spiritual advisors, close friends, or extended family members (Powers, 1991).

7.   Practitioners can assess how to best select, retain, adapt, or reject treatments by assessing the following variables on an ongoing basis: (a) capacity to implement the intervention (with or without supports), (b) contextual factors that can undermine or enhance treatment fidelity, (c) the level of strain poor progress is placing on the young child with ASD and the family as a whole, and (d) expected benefits (adapted from Powers & Handleman, 1984).

8. Practitioners should assess which factors could reduce the effectiveness of the intervention and avoid adapting these components (e.g., if dosage is critical for the expected level of change; adapted from Kumpfer, Pinyuchon, de Melo, & Whiteside, 2008).

9. A treatment may no longer have scientific evidence to support its use if adaptations are significant. Unfortunately, research rarely shows what magnitude of adaptation can maintain positive outcomes. It may be beneficial to gradually introduce a series of micro-adaptations (adapted from Kumpfer, Magalhaes, & Xie, 2012).

10. Practitioners should use language that is culturally-relevant and consider norms for role behavior (Kumpfer et al., 2012).

Note: Although the examples provided in this article focused on parents, evidence-based practitioners should consider how these same issues of cultural sensitivity and adaptation will apply to teachers, daycare workers, extended family, or others caring for children with ASD.

Author's Note:

Correspondence concerning this article should be addressed to Susan M. Wilczynski, PhD, BCBA-D, Plassman Family Distinguished Professor, Ball State University, Department of Special Education, Muncie, IN 47306, Email: smwilczynski@bsu.edu

References

American Psychiatric Association (2013). *Diagnostic and statistical manual of mental disorders* (5th ed.). Washington, D.C.: Author.

Centers for Disease Control and Prevention. (2016). Prevalence of autism spectrum disorder among children aged 8 years - autism and developmental disabilities monitoring network, 11 sites, United States, 2012. *Morbidity and Mortality Weekly Report; 63* (SS02); 1-23.

Charman, T., & Baird, G. (2002). Practitioner review: Diagnosis of autism spectrum disorder in 2-and 3-year-old children. *Journal of Child Psychology and Psychiatry, 43*(3), 289-305.

Chasson, G., Harris, G., & Neely, W. (2007). Cost comparison of early intensive behavioral intervention and special education for children with autism. *Journal of Child & Family Studies, 16*, 401-413. doi:10.1007/s10826-006-9094-1

Cidav, Z., Marcus, S. C., & Mandell, D. S. (2012). Implications of childhood autism for parental employment and earnings. *Pediatrics, 129*, 617-623.

Constantine, M. G. (2007). Microaggressions against African American clients in cross-racial counseling relationships. *Journal of Counseling Psychology, 54*, 1-16.

Dahl, N., Tervo, R., & Symons, F.J. (2007). Treatment acceptability of healthcare services for children with cerebral palsy. *Journal of Applied Research in Intellectual Disabilities, 20*(5), 475-482.

Dunlap, G., Newton, J. S., Fox, L., Benito, N., & Vaughn, B. (2001). Family involvement in functional assessment and positive behavior support. *Focus on Autism & Other Developmental Disabilities, 16*, 215-221. doi: 10.1177/108835760101600403

Dyches, T. T., Wilder, L. K., Sudweeks, R. R., Obiakor, F. E., & Algozzine, B. (2004). Multicultural issues in autism. *Journal of Autism and Developmental Disorders, 34*, 211-222.

Elliott, S. N., Turco, T. L., Evans, S., & Gresham, F. M. (1984). Group contingency interventions: Children's acceptability ratings. In *Meeting of the Association for the Advancement of Behavior Therapy,* Philadelphia.

Finn, C. A., & Sladeczek, I. E. (2001). Assessing the social validity of behavioral interventions: A review of treatment acceptability measures. *School Psychology Quarterly, 16*(2), 176.

Gengoux, G. W., Berquist, K. L., Salzman, E., Schapp, S., Phillips, J M, Fraisier... & Hardan, A. Y. (2015). Pivotal response treatment parent training for autism: Findings from a 3-month follow-up evaluation. *Journal of Autism and Developmental Disorders, 45*, 2889-2898.

Green, V., Pituch, K., Itchon, J., Choi, A., O'Reilly, M., & Sigafoos, J. (2006). Internet survey of treatments used by parents of children with autism. *Research in Developmental Disabilities, 27*, 70-84.

Guyatt, G., Cairns, J., Churchill, D., Cook, D., Haynes, B., Hirsh, J., Irvine, J., Levine, ...& Tugwell, P. (1992). Evidence-based medicine: A new approach to teaching the practice of medicine. *Journal of the American Medical Association, 17*, 2420-2425.

Heath, A. K., Ganz, J. B., Parker, R., Burke, M., & Ninci, J. (2015). A meta-analytic review of functional communication training across mode of communication, age, and disability. *Review Journal of Autism and Developmental Disorders, 2*, 155-166.

Howard, J. S., Stanislaw, H., Green, G., Sparkman, C. R., & Cohen, H. G. (2014). Comparison of behavior analytic and eclectic early interventions for young children with autism after three years. *Research in Developmental Disability, 35*, 3326-3344.

Hwang, W. (2006). The psychotherapy adaptation and modification framework. *American Psychologist, 61*, 702-715.

Jones, B. A., Dozier, C. L., & Neidert, P. L. (2014). An evaluation of the effects of access duration on preference assessment outcomes. *Journal of Applied Behavior Analysis, 47*(1), 209-213.

Koegel, R. L., Werner, G. A., Vismara, L. A., & Koegel, L. K. (2005). The effectiveness of contextually supported play date interactions between children with autism and typically developing peers. *Research & Practice for Persons with Severe Disabilties, 30*(2), 93-102.

Kumpfer, K. L., Magalhaes, C., & Xie, J. (2012). Cultural adaptations of evidence-based family interventions to strengthen families and improve children's developmental outcomes. *European Journal of Developmental Psychology, 9*(1), 104-116.

Kumpfer, K. L., Pinyuchon, M., deMelo, A., & Whiteside, H. (2008). Cultural adaption process for international dissemination of the Strengthening Families Program (SFP). *Evaluation and Health Professions, 33*(2), 226-239.

LaRoche, M. J., Davis, T. M., & D'Angelo, E. (2014). Challenges in developing a cultural evidence-based psychotherapy in the USA: Suggestions for international studies. *Australian Psychologist, 50*, 95-101.

Layer, S.A., Hanley, G.P., Heal, N.A., & Tiger, J.H. (2008). Determining individual preschoolers' preferences in a group arrangement. *Journal of Applied Behavior Analysis, 41*(1), 25-37.

Leaper, C., Anderson, K. J., & Sanders, P. (1998). Moderators of gender effects on parents' talk to their children: A meta-analysis. *Developmental Psychology, 34*, 3-27.

Matson, J. L., Kozlowski, A. M., Hattier, M. E., Horovitz, M., & Sipes, M. (2012). DSM-IV vs DSM-5 diagnostic criteria for toddlers with autism. *Developmental Neurorehabilitation, 15*, 185-190.

McConnell, S. R. (2002). Interventions to facilitate social interaction for young children with autism: Review of available research and recommendations for educational intervention and future research. *Journal of Autism and Developmental Disorders, 32*(5), 351-372.

McGee, G. G., Feldman, R. S., & Morrier, M. J. (1997). Benchmarks of social treatment for children with autism. *Journal of Autism and Developmental Disorders, 27*(4), 353-364.

Miller, D. L., & Kelley, M. L. (1992). Treatment acceptability: The effects of parent gender, marital adjustment, and child behavior. *Child and Family Behavior Therapy, 14*(1), 11-23.

Moher, D., Liberati, A., Tetzlaff, J., & Altman, D.G., The PRISMA Group (2009). Preferred reporting items for systematic reviews and meta-analyses: items for systematic reviews. *Annals of Internal Medicine, 151*(4), 264-269.

National Autism Center (2009). *National Standards Report: National Standards Project – Addressing the need for evidence-based practice guidelines for autism spectrum disorders.* Randolph, MA.

National Autism Center (2015). *Findings and conclusions: National standards project, phase 2.* Randolph, MA.

Pemberton, J. R., & Borrego, Jr, J. (2005). The relationship between treatment acceptability and familism. *International Journal of Behavioral Consultation and Therapy, 1*(4), 329.

Peters-Scheffer, N., Didden, R., Korzilius, H., & Sturney, P. (2011). A meta-analytic study on the effectiveness of comprehensive aba-based early intervention programs for children with autism spectrum disorder. *Research in Autism Spectrum Disorder, 5*, 60-69.

Poslawsky, I., Naber, F., Van Daalen, E., & Engeland, H. (2014). Parental reaction to early diagnosis of their children's autism spectrum disorder: An exploratory study. *Child Psychiatry & Human Development, 45*, 294-305.

Powers, M. D. (1991). Intervening with families of young children with severe handicaps: Contributions of a family systems approach. *School Psychology Quarterly, 6*(2), 131-146.

Powers, M. D., & Handleman, J. S. (1984). *Behavioral assessment of severe developmental disabilities.* Rockville, MD: Aspen.

Reichow, B., Barton, E., Boyd, B., & Hume, K. (2012). Early intensive behavioral intervention (EIBI) for young children with autism spectrum disorders (ASD). *Cochrane Database of Systematic Reviews, 10*, CD009260. doi:10.1002/14651858.CD009260.pub2

Richler, J., Bishop, S. L., Kleinke, J. R., & Lord, C. (2007). Restricted and repetitive behaviors in young children with autism spectrum disorders.*Journal of Autism and Developmental Disorders, 37*(1), 73-85.

Robert, S., & House, J. S. (1996). SES differentials in health by age and alternative indicators of SES. *Journal of Aging and Health, 8*(3), 359-388.

Rush, K. S., Mortenson, B. P., & Birch, S. E. (2010). Evaluation of preference assessment procedures for use with infants and toddlers. *International Journal of Behavioral Consultation and Therapy, 6*(1), 2.

Slocum, T. A., Spencer, T. D., & Detrich, R. (2012). Best available evidence: Three complementary approaches. *Education and Treatment of Children, 35*(2), 2012.

Slocum, T. A., Detrich, R., Wilczynski, S. M., Spencer, T. D., Lewis, T., & Wolfe, K. (2014). The evidence-based practice of applied behavior analysis. *The Behavior Analyst, 37*, 41-56. doi: 10.1007/s40614-014-0005-2

Smith, T. (2001). Discrete trial training in the treatment of autism. *Focus on Autism and Other Developmental Disabilities, 16*, 86-92.

Spencer, T. D., Detrich, R., & Slocum, T. A. (2012). Evidence-Based Practice: A framework for making effective decisions. *Education and Treatment of Children, 35*, 127-151.

Strauss, K., Vicari, S., Valeri, G., D'Elia, L., Arimia, S., & Fava, L. (2012). Parent inclusion in early intensive behavioral intervention: The influence of parental stress, parent treatment fidelity, and parent-mediated generalization of behavior targets on child outcomes. *Research in Developmental Disabilities, 33*, 688-703.

Tincani, M., Travers, J., & Boutot, A. (2009). Race, culture and autism spectrum disorder:Understanding the role of diversity in successful educational interventions. *Research andPractice for Persons with Severe Disabilities, 34*, 81-90.

Toussaint, K. A., Kodak, T., & Vladescu, J. C. (2016). An evaluation of choice on instructional efficacy and individual preferences among children with autism. *Journal of Applied Behavior Analysis, 49*, 170-175.

Volkmar, F., Chawarska, K., & Klin, A. (2005). Autism in infancy and early childhood. *Annual Review of Psychology, 56*, 315-356.

Wason, P. C. (1960). On the failure to eliminate hypotheses in a conceptual task. *Quarterly Journal of Experimental Psychology, 12*(3), 129-140.

Watson, L. R., Baranek, G., Crais, E. R., Reznick, S., Dykstra, J., & Perryman, T. (2007). The first year inventory: Retrospective parent responses to a questionnaire designed to identify one-year-olds at risk for autism. *Journal of Autism and Developmental Disorders, 37*, 49-61.

Weisz, J. R., Jensen-Doss, A., & Hawley, K. M. (2006). Evidence-based youth psychotherapies versus usual clinical care: A meta-analysis of direct comparisons. *American Psychologist, 61*(7), 671.

Wilczynski, S. M. (2012). Risk and strategic decision-making in developing evidence-based practice guidelines. *Education and Treatment of Children, 35*(2), 291-311.

Wong, C., Odom, S. L., Hume, K. A., Cox, A. W., Fettig, A., Kucharczyk, S....& Schultz, T. R. (2015). Evidence-based practices for children, youth, and young adults with autism spectrum disorder: A comprehensive review. *Journal of Autism and Developmental Disorders, 45*(7), 1951-1966.

Zebrowitz, L. A., Kikuchi, M., & Fellous, J. M. (2010). Facial resemblance to emotions: Group differences, impression effects, and race stereotypes. *Journal of Personality and Social Psychology, 98* (2), 175-189

List of Contributors

Jessica Bostic is a second year Ed.S student in the School Psychology program at Ball State University. Her professional interests include autism spectrum disorder, Attention-Deficit Hyperactivity Disorder, neuropsychology, gifted students, reading and behavior interventions, assessment, and motivation.

Nicole Caugherty is a school psychology doctoral student in the Department of Educational Psychology at Ball State University. Her research interests include factors influencing intervention selection, delivery, and success in the schools.

Marjorie H. Charlop, Ph.D., BCBA, has dedicated her life's work to helping children with ASD and their families. She is Professor of Psychology at Claremont McKenna College and Director of The Claremont Autism Center, her renowned research and treatment center for children with ASD and their families. As a Licensed Psychologist, she also maintains a private practice and consultation services. Dr. Charlop has hundreds of professional conference presentations and publications in the field of autism and has done workshops and lectures around the globe. Her book, "How to Treat the Child with Autism", has been translated into Spanish and Chinese. "How to Use Incidental Teaching with Autistic Spectrum Disorders" is in its second edition as Dr. Charlop works on her latest book, "Play and Social Skills for Children with ASD." Her research areas focus on the treatment of communication, motivation, social skills, and behavior problems.

Dr. Shannon Titus Dieringer is an assistant professor in the Applied Behavior Analysis Program at Ball State University. Her research focuses on motor development and physical activity of children and adolescents with autism spectrum disorder.

Neelima Duncan, Ph.D., BCBA-D, is a contract faculty in the Applied Behavior Analysis program at Ball State University. She is a licensed school psychologist and her background is in school consultation and providing early intervention services for children with autism spectrum disorder.

Jamie B. Gaither is pursuing her Educational Specialist degree in School Psychology at Ball State University. She is interested in helping to improve outcomes for children diagnosed with autism spectrum disorder (ASD). Specifically, she is interested in integrating applied behavior analytics with school curricula to help children with ASD adjust and thrive in the school setting.

Nicholas R. Harris is a school psychology doctoral student at Ball State University and received a Masters of Science degree in clinical psychology from the College of St. Joseph in Vermont. His research interestes include autism spectrum disorder, culture and diversity, evidence-based practices and assessment, and web-based training. He is working on completing his dissertation, which is titled "Cultural membership and web-based training: Does everyone really have equal access to programming?" Nicholas is currently a New York State Certified School Psychologist and upon confirmation of his doctoral degree will begin his post-doctoral training within his current district.

Amanda Henderson is a school psychology doctoral student at Ball State University. She works as a graduate assistant in Ball State's Center for Autism Spectrum Disorder. Her research interests include autism spectrum disorder and early intensive behavioral interventions.

Cathy Jones received her B.A. and M.A. from Wesleyan University and her Ph.D. from Claremont Graduate University. She is a Board Certified Behavior Analyst. She has over 15 years experience working with children with autism and other developmental disabilities in a variety of settings: research/treatment programs, public schools, and home treatment programs. Currently, Dr. Jones is an adjunct faculty member at the Chicago School of Professional Psychology.

Allyson Jordan is a third-year doctoral student in the combined Counseling Psychology/School Psychology program at the University at Buffalo. She works as a graduate assistant at the Institute for Autism Research at Canisius College assisting with implementing manualized psychosocial treatment programs for children with high-functioning autism spectrum disorder in clinic and school settings. Prior to graduate school, Allyson worked under Dr. Tristram Smith at the University of Rochester's Department of Neurodevelopmental and Behavioral Pediatrics research division on several randomized controlled trials investigating treatment for young children with autism spectrum disorder (ASD). Her current research interests include assessment and treatment of children with ASD.

Amanda Kaake is a third year graduate student in the school psychology program at Ball State University. She is completing her EdS internship at a cooperative in northeast Indiana. Her research interests include autism spectrum disorder and Applied Behavior Analysis in the school setting.

Sonia D. Kosmala is in the M.A./Ed.S. program at Ball State University. She has a Master's degree in School Psychology, and works as a graduate assistant in Ball State's Center for Autism Spectrum Disorder, as well as for the research journal, *Psychology in the Schools*.

Chris A. LaBelle, Ph.D., BCBA-D, has had over 20 years of experience serving children and adults with autism and other developmental disabilities in family home, residential home, school, and clinic-based settings. Dr. LaBelle received her bachelor's degree in psychology from the University of Florida; and subsequently received her master's and doctorate in Applied Developmental Psychology from Claremont Graduate University in California. She has presented her research at numerous conferences and has had articles published in peer reviewed journals. Her treatment focus and research interests include teaching language and social skills to individuals with autism, early intervention for children with autism, parent training, video modeling, and PECS training. Dr. LaBelle is certified in the Basic and Advanced PECS (Picture Exchange Communication System) curriculum. She served as a Visiting Assistant Professor at the University of Florida from 8/02 thru 5/04. She has also held numerous Adjunct

Faculty positions at Cal State Los Angeles, Cal State Long Beach, and University of LaVerne. She served as the Clinical Director of the Intensive Behavioral program for individuals with Prader-Willi Syndrome at the Alachua ARC and worked as a Board Certified Behavior Analyst for BASS (Behavior Analysis Support Services) in Gainesville, Florida. For the past five years, Dr. LaBelle has been residing in Millbrook, New York, raising her two young children and working as an independent consultant.

Allison C. Labrie, Ed.D, BCBA, is a contract faculty member for the Applied Behavior Analysis program at Ball State University. She primarily works and conducts research involving individuals with autism spectrum disorder, specifically she is interested in researching technology as a teaching and training tool for special educators and individuals diagnosed with autism spectrum disorder.

Constance E. McIntosh, EdD. MBA, RN, is an Assistant Professor in the School of Nursing at Ball State University. She earned her doctoral degree from Ball State University in Special Education with a cognate in nursing. Dr. McIntosh teaches in the masters' program. She teaches nursing courses in information technology courses and management/leadership; she also teaches introduction to persons with ASD in the special education department. Dr. McIntosh's line of research combines her knowledge of nursing and special education and focuses on the role of school nurses in their participation during the identification, evaluation, and treatment of children with special needs (e.g., autism spectrum disorder) and the school nurse as an essential leader of the school administrative team. She has published numerous refereed articles and has conducted national presentations.

David E. McIntosh, Ph.D., ABPP, is the David and Joanna Meeks Distinguished Professor of Special Education at Ball State. He received his PhD. (1990) from Ball State University in School Psychology. He serves as the Director of the Programs in Applied Behavior Analysis and Autism. He is the Editor-in-Chief of *Psychology in the Schools*, an interdisciplinary journal that publishes manuscripts focusing on issues confronting schools and children. Dr. McIntosh is Board Certified by the American Board of Professional Psychology, a Fellow of the American Psychological Association (Division 16), and a Fellow of the American Academy of School Psychology. He publishes extensively in the area of psychological and educational assessment of children and adolescents with learning, emotional, and/or disruptive behavior disorders. He also publishes in the area of identification and treatment of autism spectrum disorder.

Caitlin M. Pistor is a graduate student in the school psychology program at Ball State University. She has been working as a graduate assistant at BSU's Center for Autism Spectrum Disorder (CASD) for the past two years. While at CASD, Caitlin worked with Dr. Shannon Dieringer and Dr. Kimberly Zoder-Martell on a number of research projects related to the promotion of young adults and adults with ASD into the workforce, as well as understanding the impact of physical activity and motor skills on individuals with ASD. Caitlin is currently living in Indianapolis, IN, and is completing an internship in school psychology. She plans on becoming a nationally certified school psychologist working in public schools.

Kassie Shellabarger is a master's student at Ball State University and received her bachelor's degree at Butler University. She is interested in research on autism spectrum disorders in children.

Tristram Smith, Ph.D., is the Haggerty-Friedman Professor of Developmental/Behavioral Pediatric Research at the University of Rochester Medical Center (URMC), where he leads federally funded studies comparing the efficacy of different interventions for children with autism spectrum disorder (ASD). He is also a clinician in URMC's Community Consultation Program, serving students with ASD and other intellectual disabilities in schools and other agencies. His commitment to the study and treatment of children with ASD began in 1982, when he had the opportunity to volunteer as a buddy for an adult with autism who lived near his college. This experience inspired him to apply to graduate school at the University of California, Los Angeles, where he studied clinical psychology and worked as a therapist and researcher with O. Ivar Lovaas in the UCLA Young Autism Project. Before moving to Rochester in 2000, he directed clinics for children with autism and their families in the states of California, Iowa, and Washington.

Benjamin R. Thomas is Associate Clinical Director of the Claremont Autism Center, and a board certified behavior analyst. He holds a master's in psychology from Queen's College (City University of New York), and is completing his doctorate in developmental and child clinical psychology at Claremont Graduate University. He has over 15 years of experience in research, service, and training to individuals with developmental disabilities, their educators, and their families in a variety of settings.

Gabrielle Tiede is in her second year of a psychology doctoral program specializing in Intellectual and Developmental Disabilities at The Ohio State University, working under the mentorship of Dr. Katherine Walton. Prior to this placement, she worked for two years in a post-baccalaureate position in the University of Rochester's Neurodevelopmental and Behavioral Pediatrics research division. Here, she worked under Dr. Tristram Smith on several randomized controlled trials exploring the efficacy of different intervention models for children with autism spectrum disorder. Along a similar vein, her ongoing research projects at The Ohio State University focus on Naturalistic Developmental Behavioral Interventions (NDBI) for young children with autism spectrum disorder, with particular emphasis on translating evidence-based practices into community settings. In addition to her research, Gabrielle also spends time working as a graduate clinician in the Nisonger Center's School Age Autism and Developmental Clinic, and holds a teaching position in undergraduate psychology courses.

Dr. Beth A. Trammell is a licensed psychologist who specializes in working with children and families in a variety of settings. She has been in private practice for nearly 10 years, doing parent training, family therapy, individual therapy, assessment and behavior management therapy. She also has been an Assistant Professor of Psychology at Indiana University

East since 2012, teaching clinically based psychology courses online and on-campus and engaging in parent management training research projects.

Susan Wilczynski is the Plassman Family Distinguished Professor of Special Education and Applied Behavior Analysis. Before joining the faculty at Ball State University, she served as the Executive Director of the National Autism Center, where she chaired the National Standards Project. The National Standards Project was the largest comprehensive systematic review of the autism treatment literature of its time. Dr. Wilczynski developed the first center-based treatment program in the state of Nebraska while on faculty at the University of Nebraska Medical Center. As an assistant professor at the University of Southern Mississippi, she supervised the first psychology lab run by a woman in the Psychology department. Dr. Wilczynski has edited multiple books and manuals on evidence-based practice and autism. She is currently writing the book, "A practical guide to finding treatments that work for people with autism," for evidence-based practitioners of Applied Behavior Analysis. Dr. Wilczynski has published scholarly works in the *Journal of Applied Behavior Analysis*, *Behavior Modification*, *Focus on Autism and Other Developmental Disabilities*, *Educating and Treatment of Children*, and *Psychology in the Schools*. She serves as on the Practice Board for the Association for Behavior Analysis International. Dr. Wilczynski is a licensed psychologist and a board certified behavior analyst.

Kimberly A. Zoder-Martell, Ph.D., HSPP, BCBA-D, is an assistant professor in the Applied Behavior Analysis program at Ball State University. Broadly her research focuses on improving outcomes for individuals with autism spectrum disorder. She is particularly interested in strategies to train consultees to implement behavior analytic interventions with treatment fidelity.

GENERAL ARTICLE

Do Birth Complications Predict Motor Deficits in Children? The Moderating Role of Genetic and Maternal Factors

Dylan B. Jackson and Kevin M. Beaver

Abstract

A number of studies have indicated that exposure to birth complications increases the risk of fine and gross motor deficits in young children. Even so, recent research suggests children who experienced obstetrical complications differ in their degree of vulnerability to such complications. Although some scholars have theorized that genetic and maternal factors might moderate the link between birth complications and motor deficits, these possibilities have yet to be empirically tested. In the current study, we consider whether biosocial interactions between birth complications, genetic factors, and maternal factors significantly predict fine and gross motor deficits in children using data from the Early Childhood Longitudinal Study, Kindergarten Class of 1998-99 (ECLS-K), a national, longitudinal study of children.

Keywords: birth complications, fine and gross motor deficits, genetic factors, maternal depression, maternal education, moderating effects.

The main goal of the current study was to examine a number of interactions that explore the role of both genetic and maternal risk factors in moderating the effect of birth complications on fine and gross motor deficits. In recent decades, perinatal mortality has declined due partially to technological advances that facilitate the detection of complications and/or abnormalities at earlier stages of a woman's pregnancy (Dean & Davis, 2007). Consequently, a greater number of children are now surviving complications than children born in previous decades. Surviving one or more complications, however, involves a degree of neurodevelopmental risk that is often quite subtle and, as a result, may go undetected for years (du Plessis & Volpe, 2002). So although infant mortality due to perinatal complications has decreased over time, the prevalence of infants born with a greater degree of neuropsychological risk has increased (Wilson-Costello, Friedman, Minich, Fanaroff, & Hack, 2005), making the study of birth complications as a predictor of abnormal neurodevelopmental trajectories especially worthwhile.[1]

Research has revealed that one of the components of neuropsychological functioning that can be influenced by obstetrical complications are fine and gross motor deficits (Laucht, Esser, & Schmidt, 1997; Seidman et al., 2000). For example, some scholars have found infants exposed to perinatal complications (e.g., chronic hypoxia, hypoxic-ischemic complications, etc.) exhibit greater impairment in their motor skills than children who experience relatively uncomplicated births (Seidman et al., 2000). For instance, a study by Stanton, McGee, & Silva (1991) assessed the motor abilities of 476 girls and 510 boys at 5 years of age. The results indicated boys who scored higher on the perinatal complications index exhibited lower motor abilities than boys who scored lower on the index. Importantly, the index employed by Stanton et al. (1991) included a large number of complications, including, but not limited to, preterm birth, placenta previa, accidental hemorrhage, forceps, cesarean birth, breech birth, and respiratory distress. Similar findings were later obtained by Laucht et al. (1997) who found complications during pregnancy and the neonatal period were both significantly predictive of impaired motor development in offspring during preschool. Thus, it appears various labor complications can increase the risk of motor impairment in children following their birth.

A number of more recent studies have corroborated and expounded upon these results. For instance, a study by de Kieviet, Piek, Aarnoudse-Moens, and Oosterlaan (2009) recently revealed that perinatal risks associated with being born preterm or very low birth weight are predictive of significant motor impairments that persist throughout childhood. Studies using meta-analytic techniques have confirmed these patterns across a number of empirical inquiries (Geldof, Van Wassenaer, De Kieviet, Kok, & Oosterlaan, 2012). For instance, Golding, Emmett, Iles-Caven, Steer, and Lingam (2014) recently examined a host of factors that can lead to motor impairment in children. The results revealed, within their sample, children who were most at risk of motor impairment were those who were born low birth weight and/or experienced various complications or neonatal problems. Scholars have suggested that these motor impairments are the product of a reduction in the integrity of white matter and the connectivity in regions of the brain linked to movement control (Pitcher et al., 2012). Furthermore, research suggests the neurological changes that might result from a complicated birth can interfere with motor coordination into adulthood (Poole et al., 2015).

Despite the general pattern of results linking labor complications to impaired motor abilities, some researchers have suggested children who experience high-risk births vary substantially in their neuropsychological profiles by age 5, and such variation is not explained by differences in birth weight, gestational age, or medical risks at the time of birth (Lundequist, Böhm, & Smedler, 2013). Such results are consistent with the argument that infants may be differentially susceptible or resilient to perinatal risk factors (e.g., birth complications) due to genetic and/or environmental factors (Lundquist et al., 2013). Even so, research explicitly testing these arguments is lacking.

Birth Complications and Fine and Gross Motor Deficits: Is the Relationship Conditional?

The empirical evidence to date suggests obstetrical complications increase the likelihood of motor deficits for children as they develop (de Kieviet et al., 2009; Geldof et al., 2012; Golding et al., 2014; Laucht et al., 1997; Seidman et al., 2000; Stanton et al., 1991). Such complications, however, may not work in isolation to impact motor development, as research has also revealed more divergent neuromotor profiles among children who underwent high-risk births relative to children who experienced no complications (Lundequist et al., 2013). It is possible that biosocial processes, in which biological and environmental factors interact, may explain the variation in the neuromotor profiles of children who experience obstetrical complications (Beaver, DeLisi, Wright, & Vaughn, 2009; Moffitt, 2005, for examples of early biosocial processes). Although research examining genetic and maternal moderators of the link between birth complications and motor impairment has yet to be conducted, similar biosocial hypotheses have been proposed by a number of scholars examining different, yet related, outcomes. These studies underscore the relevance of both maternal factors and genetic factors in the prediction of whether birth complications will lead to developmental challenges in the long term.

Research by Raine, Brennan, and Mednick (1997), for example, has revealed birth complications are especially likely to lead to pathological violence in adulthood if the subject experienced maternal rejection early in life (e.g., unwanted pregnancy, attempt to abort the fetus). A more recent study by Arseneault, Tremblay, Boulerice, and Saucier (2002) indicates that various birth complications (e.g., fetal distress, hypoxia, umbilical cord prolapse, etc.) significantly increase childhood and adolescent violence, but only among boys who experienced adverse family environments, including low household income and low maternal education (Beck & Shaw, 2005). Other scholars have explored the moderating role of genetic factors in the link between birth complications and subsequent behavioral problems. Wichers et al. (2002), for example, examined a sample of twins and found evidence for a negative gene-environment interaction wherein a latent measure of genetic risk was less relevant for low birth-weight children relative to normal-weight children in the formation of childhood problem behaviors. An earlier study by Milberger, Biederman, Faraone, Guite, and Tsuang (1997), however, found no evidence for such an interaction. Recent research employing a within-family design has also revealed that latent measures of genetic risk and labor complications interact to increase the risk of schizophrenia (Forsyth et al., 2013).

Despite the evidence for differential susceptibility to birth complications in the case of violence, behavioral problems, and schizophrenia, no research to date has tested whether a similar process is occurring in the development of motor skills during early childhood. Considering 1) the large body of work linking obstetrical complications to motor impairment, 2) the evidence for differential vulnerability to the influence of birth complications on motor impairment, and 3) the relevance of genetic and maternal factors in moderating the influence of birth complications on other developmental outcomes, we propose the following hypotheses. First, we propose that a greater number of birth complications will be associated with greater fine and gross motor deficits. Second, we propose that birth complications will interact with maternal depression, maternal education, and genetic risk to predict fine and gross motor skills. We aim to test these hypotheses in the present study using a nationally representative sample of children.

Method

Sample

The present study used data from the Early Childhood Longitudinal Study, Kindergarten Class of 1998-1999 (ECLS-K). The study, with an initial sample size of approximately 21,000 children, is one of the largest nationally representative studies of U.S. children. The ECLS-K employed a multistage probability sampling design, sampling U.S. counties, then schools within the counties, then children within the schools. The primary objective of the ECLS-K was to examine children's educational, cognitive, and social development from kindergarten through eighth grade. This was accomplished though assessments and telephone interviews conducted by trained evaluators, in addition to garnering data from children's birth certificates. Since the first wave of data collection, which took place in the 1998-1999 school year, six additional waves of data have been collected. The first two waves were collected during the fall and spring of the 1998-1999 school year, when the children were approximately six years old. During the fall and spring of the 1999-2000 school year (i.e., first grade), waves three and four of the data collection took place. Waves five, six, and seven were measured during the third, fifth and eighth grades respectively. Thus, by the final wave, subjects were roughly 14 years of age.

A unique feature of the ECLS-K is that when a twin respondent was identified, their co-twin was subsequently added to the study and subjected to similar assessments and data collection procedures. A sizeable number of twins [N = 360; 118 monozygotic (MZ), 242 dizygotic (DZ)] were ultimately included in the study at the first wave of data collection. Importantly, although the parents of twins in the sample were asked about complications that each of their twins may have experienced during delivery, parents of singletons were not asked such questions. Furthermore, the availability of the twin subsample permits us to a) account for the genetic similarity of subjects and b) effectively examine whether genetic risk interacts with perinatal experiences to predict motor deficits in early childhood. Since these objectives are compatible with our research agenda, the present analysis is limited to an examination of data collected from the subsample of twins within the ECLS-K study.

Measures

Outcome Measures

Fine motor deficits. Our measure of fine motor deficits was derived from the Early Screening Inventory – Revised (ESI-R; Meisels, Marsden, Wiske, & Henderson, 1997). Prior research has indicated that the ESI-R is a reliable and valid indicator of both fine and gross motor ability (Grissmer, Grim, Aiyer, Murrah, & Steele, 2010; Son & Meisels, 2006), which makes it well-suited to the current study.

In order to estimate their fine motor ability, children were asked to copy five simple figures, build a gate, and draw a person during the first wave of data collection (when they were approximately six years old). Children were scored using a range of 0-2, with higher scores reflecting more advanced fine motor ability. Children's composite fine motor ability scores were reverse-coded so that subjects evincing the greatest fine motor deficits received higher scores. See Table 1 for descriptive statistics related to the fine motor deficits as well as all of the other variables/scales used in the analyses.

Table 1:
Descriptive Statistics for ECLS-K Twin Subsample

Variable	Mean	Standard Deviation	Range
Fine Motor Deficits	3.49	2.07	0-9
Gross Motor Deficits	1.82	1.89	0-9
Fine and Gross Motor Deficits	0	.81	-1.32-3.28
Total Birth Complications	.60	1.09	0-6
Genetic Risk	.84	.70	0-3
Maternal Education	4.26	1.79	1-9
Maternal Depression	1.45	.45	1-3.67
Parental Withdrawal	1.56	.44	1-3
Parental Involvement	2.78	.50	1-4
Parental Affection	3.69	.39	1.25-4
Corporal Punishment	.21	.41	0-1
Neighborhood Disadvantage	1.12	.20	1-2.33
Age	6.22	.36	5.47-7.29
Sex (Male = 1)	.42	.49	0-1
Race (Non-White = 1)	.38	.49	0-1

Gross motor deficits. The gross motor skills of each child were also assessed at wave 1. Specifically, children were asked to engage in a number of tasks, including balancing, walking backward, hopping, and skipping. Scores on these items also ranged from 0 to 2, with higher scores signifying greater gross motor ability. Children's composite gross motor ability scores were reverse-coded so that subjects evincing more gross motor deficits received higher scores.

Fine and gross motor deficits. The study followed the lead of prior research (Jackson & Beaver, 2013; Laucht et al., 1997) and created a combined measure of fine and gross motor deficits in order to tap the extent to which the children evinced more extensive motor deficits across larger and smaller muscle groups. This measure was created by standardizing and summing together the measures of fine and gross motor deficits. Importantly, these indicators of motor functioning were only assessed during the kindergarten school year. As a result, the researchers were unable to test changes in motor impairment over time.

Perinatal and Genetic Measures

Total birth complications. The ECLS-K is a particularly rich source of data that measures prenatal and perinatal experiences. For the twin subsample, particularly useful details concerning the mother's pregnancy and her birthing experience were obtained. Mothers of the participants were asked to indicate whether a number of specific birth complications occurred during their pregnancy and/ or delivery. The birth complications measured range from mildly serious to severe, and include respiratory distress of the neonate, fetal distress, premature birth, breech birth, anoxia, the presence of moderate to heavy meconium, cesarean delivery, eclampsia, premature membrane rupture, and dysfunctional labor.

Some studies using the ECLS-K have examined the effects of each complication individually (e.g., Beaver & Wright, 2005). However, the current study took a different approach in measuring birth complications. The various labor complications were dummy coded and subsequently summed so that mother-child dyads who experienced a greater number of total complications scored higher on this item.[2] Similar additive measures have been utilized in recent research examining the impact of perinatal experiences on the subsequent functioning of children (Favaro, Tenconi, Bosello, Degortes, & Santonastaso, 2011; Johnson, LaPrairie, Brennan, Stowe, & Newport, 2012; Young, Riordan, & Stark, 2011). One of the virtues of a cumulative measure of perinatal risk is its ability to capture a child's exposure to a large spectrum of adverse delivery conditions. Furthermore, research has suggested that the effects of labor complications on child development may be especially potent as such complications coalesce in a particular birthing experience, such that the child who is exposed to multiple complications may be especially at risk for various negative outcomes (Bradley, Caldwell, Rock, Casey, & Nelson, 1987; McNeil et al., 2000; Prechtl, 1968), including motor deficits (Stanton, McGee, & Silva, 1991).

Genetic risk. The study followed the lead of prior research (Beaver et al., 2009; Jaffee et al., 2005) in creating our latent measure of genetic risk. We first sorted the twins into pairs. Next, one twin from each pair was randomly chosen as the target twin and the other twin in the pair was then designated as the co-twin. Subsequently, each co-twin's motor deficits score was transformed into a dichotomous variable that identifies the co-twins with particularly poor motor ability.[3] Co-twins who scored at or above the 90th percentile on the motor deficits index were coded as "1", whereas co-twins who scored below the 90th percentile on the motor deficits index were coded as "0". The genetic risk of each target twin was then modeled as a function of both their co-twin's score on the dichotomous motor deficits variable as well as their zygosity (Beaver et al., 2009; Jaffee et al., 2005).

Ultimately, the genetic risk scale that was constructed for the target twins in the present study ranged from 0-3, with higher scores reflecting a greater degree of genetic risk. To be precise, MZ target twins whose co-twin scored "0" on the dichotomous motor deficits variable were coded as a "0" on the genetic risk scale, DZ target twins whose co-twin scored "0" on the dichotomous motor deficits variable were coded as a "1" on the genetic risk scale, DZ target twins whose co-twin scored "1" on the dichotomous motor deficits variable were coded as a "2" on the genetic risk scale, and MZ target twins whose co-twin scored "1" on the dichotomous motor deficits variable were coded as a "3" on the genetic risk scale.

Maternal Traits

Maternal education. Information concerning the educational achievement of the participants' mothers was also available in the ECLS-K. During the first wave of data collection, parents were asked about their years of completed schooling. Mothers' values on this item ranged from 1 (8th grade or below) to 9 (doctorate or professional degree).

Maternal depression. In addition to the extent of formal education received by the mother, her level of depressive symptomatology was also assessed. Items tapping the mothers' experience with depression were available during several waves of data collection, including the second wave. Specifically, parents were asked 12 questions concerning their psychological well-being, including questions about how frequently they felt unusually bothered by things, depressed, lonely, unmotivated, and unfocused. Other questions concerning poor sleep and appetite were also asked. Response options include 1 (never), 2 (some of the time), 3 (a moderate amount of the time), and 4 (most of the time). High scores are indicative of a greater degree of maternal depressive symptomatology at wave 2. The 12 items were summed to form the maternal depression index coefficient (alpha coefficient = .86).

Socialization Measures

Parental withdrawal. We also included several dimensions of parenting as covariates in our analysis, including indicators of parental withdrawal (Beaver, Wright, & DeLisi, 2007; Jackson &

Beaver, 2013). At wave 2, parents were asked if they felt trapped in their role, if they felt it was more work than pleasure, if they felt too busy to be a parent, if they felt that they were sacrificing their life to be a parent, and if they felt angry in their role as a parent. Responses for these items include 1 (completely true), 2 (mostly true), 3 (somewhat true), and 4 (not true at all). In order to tap parental withdrawal, items were reverse-coded and then summed to create a scale coefficient (alpha coefficient = .77).

Parental involvement. During the first wave of data collection, a number of questions were asked about the types of activities parents engage in on a regular basis with their child. In particular, parents were asked how many times per week they read to their child, sang songs with their child, helped their child with chores, told stories to their child, played games with their child, helped their child with art projects, played sports with their child, taught their child about nature, and helped their child build things. Response options included 1 (not at all), 2 (once or twice), 3 (three to six times), and 4 (everyday). All of the items were summed to create a parental involvement scale coefficient (alpha coefficient = .74).

Parental affection. At the second wave of data collection, parents were asked if they always showed love toward their child, if they frequently expressed their affection for their child (e.g. kiss, hug), if they felt liked by their child, and if they frequently enjoyed warm interactions with their child. Items include 1 (completely true), 2 (mostly true), 3 (somewhat true), and 4 (not true at all). The four items were reverse-coded and added together to create the parental affection index, for which higher scores reflect higher levels of parental affection coefficient (alpha coefficient = .68).

Corporal punishment. A dichotomous item tapping the parent's physical punishment of their child was also incorporated into the analysis. Parents were asked at wave 2 about how they would respond in a hypothetical scenario in which their child hit them. Parents who stated that they would hit or spank their child in response to the child's behavior were coded as "1". If the parents said that they would react using another type of non-physical punishment, they were coded as "0". Thus, higher scores on this item are reflective of a greater willingness of the parent to resort to physical punishment as a method of disciplining their child.

Neighborhood disadvantage. In addition to several variables measuring parenting behaviors, we also included a measure of each respondent's neighborhood context. At wave 2, parents were asked concerning the overall safety and desirability of their neighborhood. Specifically, parents were asked six questions concerning how safe it was for their child to play outside, whether people were selling drugs or using alcohol in the neighborhood, the extent of violent crime in the neighborhood (including burglaries and robberies), whether there were vacant houses nearby, and whether the streets were littered with trash. Values on each item included 1 (item is a big problem), 2 (item is somewhat of a problem), and 3 (item is not a problem). Items were then reverse-coded so that higher scores were indicative of greater neighborhood disadvantage. The six items were subsequently summed to create an index of neighborhood disadvantage coefficient (alpha = .65).

Control Variables

Finally, measures of age, race, and sex of the child were also included in the analysis as controls. Each model includes a dichotomous race variable (1 = non-white, 0 = white), a dichotomous sex variable (1 = male, 0 = female), and a continuous age variable, all of which were measured at the first wave of data collection.[4]

Analysis

The research estimated ordinary least squares (OLS) regression models to examine the association between birth complications and motor deficits. The first set of models examined whether total birth complications was significantly predictive of fine motor deficits in children. The second set of models tested the possibility that birth complications might be significantly predictive of gross motor deficits. Finally, the last set of models explored the role of birth complications in predicting scores on the combined motor deficits measure. An important subset of models examined whether genetic and maternal factors might moderate any direct effect of total birth complications on motor impairment.

As mentioned previously, the analysis was confined to the subsample of twins included in the ECLS-K, as these were the only subjects for whom data regarding birth complications are available. Furthermore, due to the limited size of the twin sample, as well as the discontinuation of the motor skills measures, our analysis only contains data from the kindergarten school year (waves 1 and 2). Importantly, the researchers followed the lead of previous researchers (Beaver et al., 2009) and randomly selected one twin (the target twin) from each twin pair to be included in the final analysis.[5] After making these necessary adjustments, final analytical sample sizes ranged between 150 and 155 participants across models.

Results

The analysis began by calculating descriptive statistics of all of the variables included in the study. Importantly, the sample was 42% male, 38% nonwhite, and approximately six years of age when motor skills were assessed. Subsequently, multivariate regression models were estimated to examine the role of total birth complications in predicting fine and gross motor deficits. Table 2 presents the results of the regression equations predicting fine motor deficits. Models 1, 2, and 3 display the findings for the main effects models, whereas models 4, 5, and 6 display the findings for the models containing interaction terms. The results reveal exposure to a greater number of birth complications significantly increases the risk of fine motor deficits during the kindergarten school year, controlling for various social and demographic factors ($b = .19$, $p < .05$). Importantly, none of the socialization variables had a significant effect on fine motor deficits. However, maternal education was associated with a significant decrease in fine motor deficits (b = -.34, p < .05). Furthermore, the results from the last three models indicate the effect of birth complications on fine motor impairment is not significantly moderated by genetic risk, maternal depression, or maternal education.

Table 3 displays the findings of the regression equations predicting gross motor deficits. Again, models 1, 2, and 3 show the findings for the main effects models, whereas models 4, 5, and 6 display the findings for the models containing interaction terms. The main effects models demonstrate that, in contrast to the fine

Table 2:
The Direct and Interactive Effects of Total Birth Complications, Genetic Risk, Maternal Depression, and Maternal Education on Fine Motor Deficits in Children

| | Fine Motor Deficits | | | | | |
| | Model 1 | Model 2 | Model 3 | Model 4 | Model 5 | Model 6 |
	b/Beta	b/Beta	b/Beta	b/Beta	b/Beta	b/Beta
Total Birth Complications	.19* .19	NA	.18* .18	.18* .18	.21* .22	.14 .15
	(.08)		(.08)	(.08)	(.08)	(.08)
Genetic Risk	NA	.15 .16	.15 .16	.15 .16	.15 .16	.14 .15
		(.08)	(.08)	(.08)	(.08)	(.08)
Age	-.18* -.18	-.12 -.13	-.13 -.13	-.13 -.13	-.11* -.11	-.13 -.14
	(.08)	(.08)	(.08)	(.08)	(.08)	(.08)
Sex	-.11 -.06	-.19 -.09	-.16 -.08	-.16 -.08	-.20 .10	-.17 -.09
	(.16)	(.16)	(.16)	(.16)	(.16)	(.16)
Race (non-white)	-.16 -.08	-.19 -.09	-.11 -.05	-.11 -.05	-.10 -.05	-.12 -.06
	(.18)	(.18)	(.18)	(.18)	(.18)	(.18)
Neighborhood Disadvantage	-.07 -.07	-.07 -.07	-.07 -.07	-.07 -.07	-.07 -.07	-.08 -.08
	(.08)	(.08)	(.08)	(.08)	(.08)	(.08)
Maternal Education	-.34* -.33	-.31* -.31	-.33* -.32	-.33* -.32	-.34* -.33	-.33* -.33
	(.09)	(.09)	(.09)	(.09)	(.09)	(.09)
Maternal Depression	-.03 -.03	-.01 -.01	-.04 -.04	-.04 -.04	-.05 -.05	-.03 -.03
	(.09)	(.09)	(.09)	(.09)	(.09)	(.09)
Parental Withdrawal	-.04 -.03	-.05 -.05	-.05 -.05	-.05 -.05	-.04 -.04	-.04 -.04
	(.09)	(.09)	(.09)	(.09)	(.09)	(.09)
Parental Involvement	.15 .14	.16 .16	.13 .13	.13 .13	.13 .12	.15 .15
	(.09)	(.09)	(.09)	(.09)	(.09)	(.09)
Parental Affection	-.10 -.10	-.12 -.12	-.12 -.13	-.12 -.13	-.11 -.11	-.12 -.12
	(.08)	(.08)	(.08)	(.08)	(.09)	(.08)
Corporal Punishment	.10 .10	.10 .10	.10 .10	.10 .10	.11 .11	.10 .10
	(.08)	(.09)	(.09)	(.09)	(.09)	(.08)
Total Birth Comp. X Genetic Risk	NA	NA	NA	-.01 -.01 (.07)	NA	NA
Total Birth Comp. X Maternal Depression	NA	NA	NA	NA	-.11 -.11 (.08)	NA
Total Birth Comp. X Maternal Ed.	NA	NA	NA	NA	NA	.15 .14 (.08)
N	152	151	150	150	150	150
R²	.19	.18	.21	.21	.22	.23

motor deficits models, the total number of birth complications did not significantly predict gross motor impairment. Nevertheless, a higher level of genetic risk significantly increased the likelihood of developing gross motor deficits by early childhood (b = .22, p < .05). Although a significant genetic effect was detected, none of the socialization or maternal variables reached statistical significance in the main effects models. Finally, the interaction between total birth complications and genetic risk (displayed in model 4) did not emerge as statistically significant. However, maternal depression and maternal education emerged as significant moderators of the

Table 3:
The Direct and Interactive Effects of Total Birth Complications, Genetic Risk, Maternal Depression, and Maternal Education on Gross Motor Deficits in Children

| | Gross Motor Deficits | | | | | |
	Model 1	Model 2	Model 3	Model 4	Model 5	Model 6
	b/Beta	b/Beta	b/Beta	b/Beta	b/Beta	b/Beta
Total Birth Complications	.13 .13	NA	.12 .13	.12 .12	.20* .20	.07 .07
	(.08)		(.08)	(.08)	(.08)	(.08)
Genetic Risk	NA	.22* .23	.22* .22	.24* .25	.22* .23	.21* .21
		(.08)	(.08)	(.08)	(.08)	(.08)
Age	-.24* -.25	-.21* -.22	-.22* -.23	-.22* -.22	-.19* -.20	-.23* -.23
	(.08)	(.08)	(.08)	(.08)	(.08)	(.08)
Sex	.33* .17	.26 .14	.29 .15	.25 .13	.22 .11	.28 .14
	(.17)	(.16)	(.16)	(.17)	(.16)	(.16)
Race (non-white)	-.28 -.14	-.31 -.16	-.27 -.13	-.29 -.14	-.26 -.13	-.27 -.13
	(.18)	(.18)	(.18)	(.18)	(.18)	(.17)
Neighborhood Disadvantage	.07 .07	.07 .07	.07 .07	.06 .07	.06 .07	.05 .05
	(.08)	(.08)	(.08)	(.08)	(.08)	(.08)
Maternal Education	-.01 -.01	.01 .01	-.01 -.01	.00 .00	-.04 -.04	-.02 -.02
	(.09)	(.09)	(.09)	(.09)	(.09)	(.08)
Maternal Depression	.01 .01	.00 .00	-.02 -.02	-.03 -.03	-.05 -.06	.00 .00
	(.10)	(.09)	(.09)	(.09)	(.09)	(.09)
Parental Withdrawal	-.01 -.01	.01 .01	.01 .01	.02 .02	.02 .02	.03 .03
	(.10)	(.09)	(.09)	(.09)	(.09)	(.09)
Parental Involvement	.03 .03	.07 .07	.06 .06	.06 .06	.05 .06	.09 .09
	(.09)	(.08)	(.08)	(.08)	(.08)	(.08)
Parental Affection	.10 .11	.07 .07	.07 .07	.08 .08	.09 .09	.07 .08
	(.08)	(.08)	(.08)	(.08)	(.08)	(.08)
Corporal Punishment	-.12 -.12	-.09 -.10	-.09 -.10	-.07 -.08	-.07 -.08	-.09 -.09
	(.09)	(.08)	(.08)	(.08)	(.08)	(.08)
Total Birth Comp. X Genetic Risk	NA	NA	NA	-.09 -.09 (.08)	NA	NA
Total Birth Comp. X Maternal Depression	NA	NA	NA	NA	-.21* -.21 (.09)	NA
Total Birth Comp. X Maternal Ed.	NA	NA	NA	NA	NA	.24* .23 (.08)
N	153	152	151	151	151	151
R^2	.11	.15	.17	.18	.21	.21

effect of birth complications on gross motor deficits (b = -.21, p < .05; b = .24, p < .05). The results suggest that the number of birth complications is more relevant to the development of gross motor impairment for individuals whose mothers a) exhibit less depressive symptomatology and b) attained more education.

Finally, displayed on Table 4 are the results from six models examining the association between total birth complications and the composite motor deficits measure. The results show that both genetic risk and number of birth complications significantly increased the likelihood of exhibiting motor impairment in early childhood (b = .16, p < .05; b = .17, p < .05). Furthermore, none of

Table 4:
The Direct and Interactive Effects of Total Birth Complications, Genetic Risk, Maternal Depression, and Maternal Education on Fine and Gross Motor Deficits in Children

	Fine and Gross Motor Deficits					
	Model 1	Model 2	Model 3	Model 4	Model 5	Model 6
	b/Beta	b/Beta	b/Beta	b/Beta	b/Beta	b/Beta
Total Birth Complications	.16* .20	NA	.17* .20	.15* .18	.21* .26	.12 .14
	(.07)		(.07)	(.06)	(.07)	(.07)
Genetic Risk	NA	.15* .18	.16* .19	.19* .23	.15* .19	.14* .17
		(.07)	(.06)	(.06)	(.06)	(.06)
Age	-.24* -.28	-.21* -.25	-.21* -.25	-.23* -.27	-.19* -.23	-.22* -.26
	(.07)	(.07)	(.07)	(.07)	(.07)	(.07)
Sex	.17 .10	.12 .07	.14 .09	.10 .06	.09 .06	.14 .08
	(.14)	(.14)	(.14)	(.13)	(.14)	(.13)
Race (non-white)	-.24 -.13	-.29 -.16	-.22 -.13	-.22 -.13	-.21 -.12	-.22 -.13
	(.15)	(.15)	(.15)	(.15)	(.15)	(.15)
Neighborhood Disadvantage	.00 .00	-.01 -.01	-.01 -.01	-.02 -.02	-.01 -.01	-.02 -.03
	(.07)	(.07)	(.07)	(.07)	(.07)	(.07)
Maternal Education	-.17* -.20	-.16* -.18	-.18* -.20	-.17* -.20	-.20* -.23	-.18* -.21
	(.07)	(.07)	(.07)	(.07)	(.07)	(.07)
Maternal Depression	-.01 -.01	.01 .01	-.02 -.03	-.03 -.04	-.04 -.05	-.01 -.01
	(.08)	(.08)	(.08)	(.08)	(.08)	(.08)
Parental Withdrawal	-.03 -.03	-.04 -.04	-.03 -.03	-.02 -.03	-.03 -.03	-.02 -.02
	(.08)	(.08)	(.07)	(.07)	(.07)	(.07)
Parental Involvement	.08 .10	.11 .13	.09 .11	.11 .13	.09 .10	.12 .14
	(.07)	(.07)	(.07)	(.07)	(.07)	(.07)
Parental Affection	.01 .02	.01 .01	.00 .00	.02 .02	.02 .02	.01 .01
	(.07)	(.07)	(.07)	(.07)	(.07)	(.06)
Corporal Punishment	-.02 -.03	-.01 -.01	.00 .00	.01 .01	.01 .01	.00 .00
	(.07)	(.07)	(.07)	(.07)	(.07)	(.07)
Total Birth Comp. X Genetic Risk	NA	NA	NA	-.15* -.19	NA	NA
				(.06)		
Total Birth Comp. X Maternal Depression	NA	NA	NA	NA	-.16* -.18	NA
					(.07)	
Total Birth Comp. X Maternal Ed.	NA	NA	NA	NA	NA	.18* .20
						(.07)
N	155	155	154	154	154	154
R²	.15	.15	.18	.22	.21	.22

the maternal or socialization variables significantly influenced the development of motor deficits, except for maternal education. In the final three models, all interaction terms emerged as significant (b = -.15, p < .05; b = -.16, p < .05; b = .18, p < .05). As demonstrated in Figure 1, individuals who scored higher on genetic risk (e.g., 1 standard deviation above the mean) were less likely to evince poorer motor functioning in response to a greater number of birth complications. Conversely, when genetic risk is particularly low (e.g., one standard deviation below the mean), then exposure to additional birth complications significantly increases the likelihood of incurring additional motor deficits. Similar patterns emerged in the interaction between birth complications and maternal depression (see figure 2) as well as the interaction between birth complications and maternal education (see figure 3). In short, the positive effect of total birth complications on motor deficits is significantly reduced among subjects whose mothers exhibit high depressive symptomatology and is significantly enhanced among subjects with more educated mothers. Thus, exposure to a greater number of birth complications appears to be more consequential for the motor abilities of subjects who possess a lower degree of maternal risk.[6]

Discussion

This study used a sample of twins to assess the role of birth complications in predicting motor deficits during childhood. It also tested whether genetic factors and maternal characteristics moderated the effect of birth complications on motor deficits. Three key findings emerged. First, exposure to a greater number of birth complications was found to significantly increase the likelihood of exhibiting motor deficits, particularly fine motor deficits, during childhood (yielding partial support for our first hypothesis). Our results corroborate the findings of previous research suggesting that the detrimental effects of obstetrical complications may be particularly potent as perinatal insults accumulate (Bradley et al.,

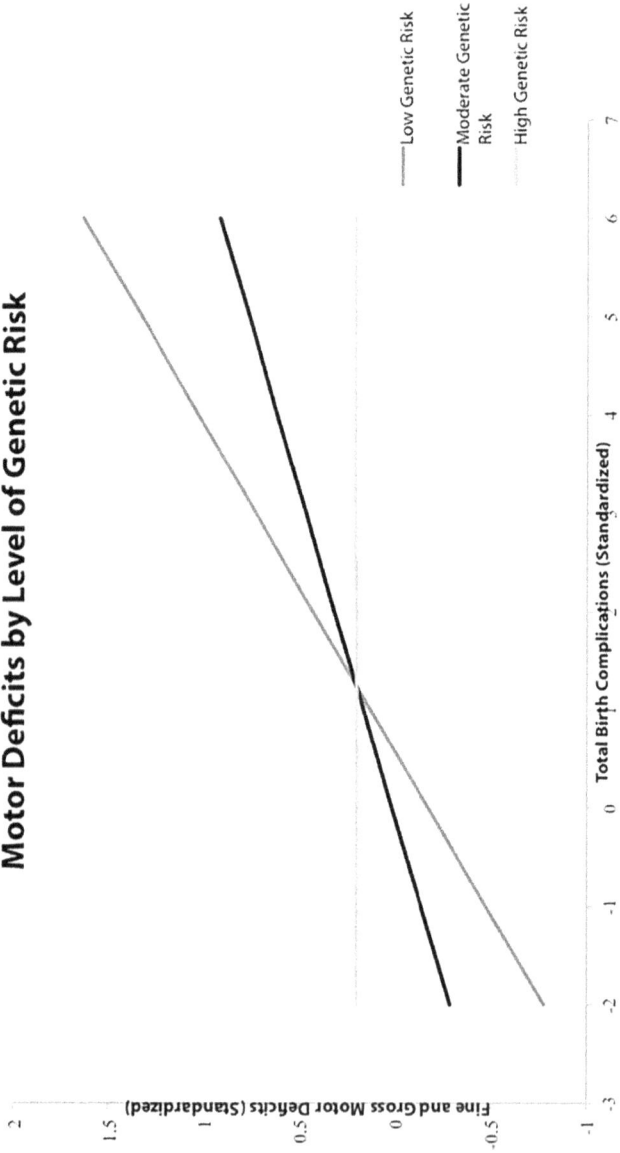

Figure 1:
The Impact of Total Birth Complications on Fine and Gross
Motor Deficits by Level of Genetic Risk

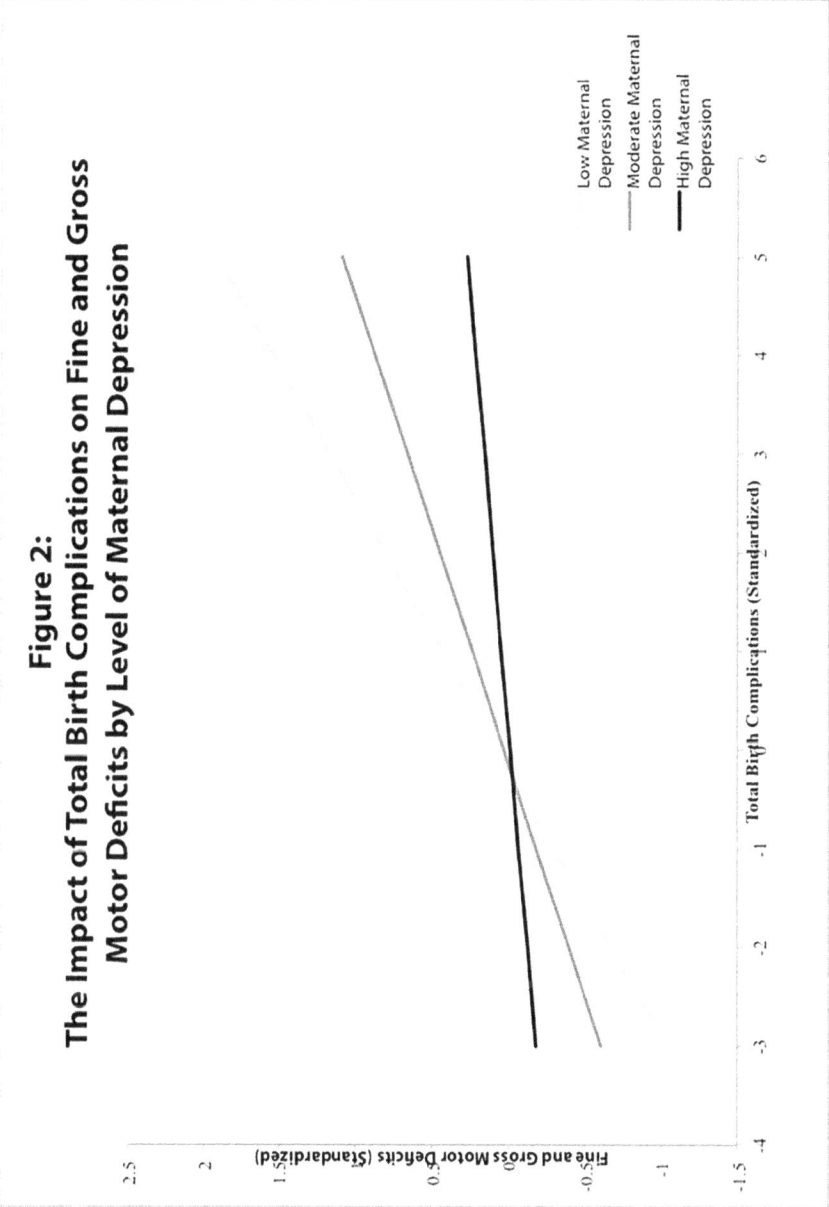

Figure 2:
The Impact of Total Birth Complications on Fine and Gross
Motor Deficits by Level of Maternal Depression

Figure 3:
The Impact of Total Birth Complications on Fine and Gross Motor Deficits by Level of Maternal Education

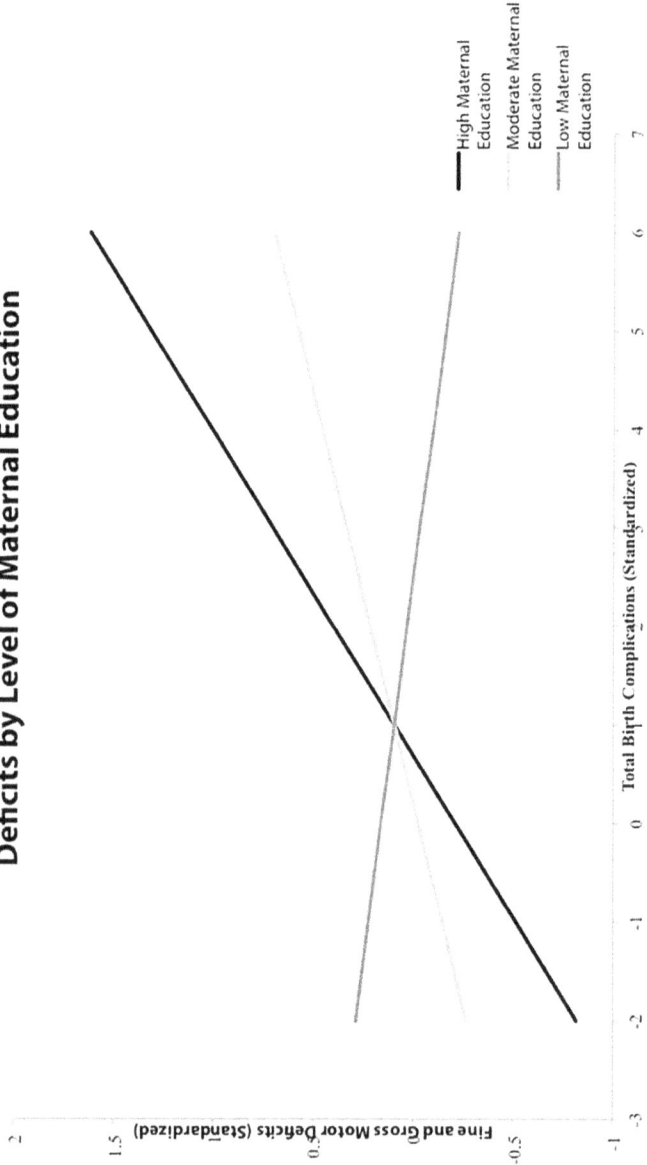

1987; McNeil et al., 2000; Prechtl, 1968; Stanton, McGee, & Silva, 1991).

Second, although genetic factors appear to play a significant role in the development of gross motor impairment during childhood, the effects of several parenting measures (e.g., parental involvement, parental attachment) on motor functioning were consistently null. The only social risk factor for the development of motor deficits that emerged was the level of education attained by the child's mother. The third key finding of the current study was that maternal education, maternal depression, and genetic risk all significantly moderated the association between birth complications and motor deficits (yielding support for hypotheses 2, 3, and 4). In all three cases, the results indicated that the effect of birth complications on motor deficits was more potent for those children who were a) at low genetic risk and/or b) low maternal risk.

A wealth of research has found evidence for various types of biosocial processes in which genetic, social, and non-social environments interact to predict negative child outcomes (Beaver et al., 2009; Raine, 2002; Raine et al., 1997; Wichers et al., 2002). One possible explanation of the interactive patterns detected in our study can be found in the social push perspective (Raine, 2002). Under this perspective, physiological, biological, and genetic risk factors are expected to predispose children to negative outcomes the most when social "pushes" toward such outcomes are lacking. Conversely, when social risks are prevalent, they are expected to camouflage the contribution of biological risks to child outcomes (Raine, 2002). The results of the present study are consistent with the "social push" hypothesis concerning biosocial interactions, as psychophysiological factors (e.g., birth complications) were found to exert their greatest effects among more socially privileged populations (i.e., children of highly educated mothers) or under more socially advantageous conditions (i.e., children whose mothers reported few, if any, depressive symptoms). Our study also revealed that the influence of genetic risk on motor deficits was more potent among subjects with more fortunate birthing experiences, which is also consistent with the social push perspective (Raine, Reynolds, Venables, & Mednick, 1997; Wichers et al., 2002).

The limitations of the study should be mentioned. First, a small number of biosocial interactions was tested, despite the potentially large number of relevant interactions. Future research should consider additional environments that might moderate the effects of birth complications on child motor impairment, including non-home environments. Second, the sample was limited to twins in order to facilitate a genetically sensitive analysis. Although the inclusion of a genetic risk measure contributes to the internal validity of the study, the generalizability of the results to the broader population of singletons cannot be guaranteed.[7] It should be noted, however, that a recent study by Barnes and Boutwell (2013) suggests twin research is likely more generalizable than previously assumed.

Third, the data, while comprehensive, are slightly dated, as the participants were born in 2001. Although it is difficult to definitively say that these results are applicable at the current time, there is no clear rationale as to why they would not be, particularly as more and more children are surviving labor complications than in years past (Dean & Davis, 2007). Fourth, much of the variance in motor deficits is left unexplained by the models, despite a sizeable increase in the portion of the variance explained once the interaction terms were added to the models. Finally, due to the limitations in the size of the twin sample and the measurement of motor deficits, the researchers were unable to extend the analysis to subsequent waves of the ECLS-K. It would have been useful to examine whether the effect of birth complications on motor deficits persisted into early adolescence. Future research should explore the risk of motor deficits during later life stages for individuals exposed to birth complications.[8]

In sum, deficits in motor functioning during childhood appear to be influenced by a confluence of biological, genetic, and social factors. As the present study indicated, obstetrical complications contribute to an individual's risk of exhibiting motor deficits, and the extent of risk seems to vary based on genetic and social circumstances. Additional empirical examinations of the role of birth complications in the development of persistent motor deficits would be worthwhile, particularly since motor deficits during childhood have been found to increase the probability of various negative outcomes, including low self-control and conduct problems (Jackson & Beaver, 2013). Additional research in this area will hopefully facilitate a better understanding of how to identify at-risk children and intervene at the earliest stages of the life course, thereby improving their overall quality of life.

NOTES

1. Technological advances have also gone hand in hand with an increase in the rate of multiple births (e.g., twins). Research has revealed that since the 1980s, this increase in the rate of multiple births has contributed to the rise in overall rates of preterm delivery (Blondel et al., 2002).

2. Importantly, twins born to the same mother may or may not experience the same number of complications, and thus may have different scores on this item.

3. Whether fine motor, gross motor, or combined motor deficits were used in the creation of the genetic risk measure was contingent on the model and its corresponding outcome variable. For instance, in the models examining fine motor deficits as the outcome variable, scores on the fine motor deficit index were used to create the genetic risk scale.

4. Alternative measures of race/ethnicity do not alter the findings of the present study in any substantive way.

5. The inclusion of only one twin from each twin pair in the final sample ensures that the Ordinary Least Squares assumption of independent observations is not violated.

6. It is important to note that, although the proportion of the variance in the outcome explained by the direct effects models is relatively low in the combined motor deficits models ($R^2 = .15$), it increases by approximately 50% ($R^2 = .22$ or $.23$) when the interactions of interest are included. Also, Bonferroni's correction reveals that the results of the interaction models remain significant after adjusting for multiple tests.

7. This may be particularly relevant in the case of birth complications, as twins are at higher risk of a number of complications related to preterm delivery (Blondel et al., 2002).

8. Research employing relevant genetic polymorphisms would also be useful as a way to test the replicability of the present findings.

References

Arseneault, L., Tremblay, R. E., Boulerice, B., & Saucier, J. F. (2002). Obstetrical complications and violent delinquency: Testing two developmental pathways. *Child Development, 73*(2), 496-508.

Barnes, J. C., & Boutwell, B. B. (2013). A demonstration of the generalizability of twin-based research on antisocial behavior. *Behavior Genetics, 43*(2), 1-12.

Beaver, K. M., DeLisi, M., Wright, J. P., & Vaughn, M. G. (2009). Gene-environment interplay and delinquent involvement evidence of direct, indirect, and interactive effects. *Journal of Adolescent Research, 24*(2), 147-168.

Beaver, K. M., & Wright, J. P. (2005). Evaluating the effects of birth complications on low self-control in a sample of twins. *International Journal of Offender Therapy and Comparative Criminology, 49*(4), 450-471.

Beaver, K. M., Wright, J. P., & Delisi, M. (2007). Self-control as an executive function: Reformulating Gottfredson and Hirschi's parental socialization thesis. *Criminal Justice and Behavior, 34*, 1345-1361.

Beck, J. E., & Shaw, D. S. (2005). The influence of perinatal complications and environmental adversity on boys' antisocial behavior. *Journal of Child Psychology and Psychiatry, 46*(1), 35-46.

Blondel, B., Kogan, M. D., Alexander, G. R., Dattani, N., Kramer, M. S., Macfarlane, A., & Wen, S. W. (2002). The impact of the increasing number of multiple births on the rates of preterm birth and low birthweight: an international study. *American Journal of Public Health, 92*(8), 1323-1330.

Bradley, R. H., Caldwell, B. M., Rock, S. L., Casey, P. M., & Nelson, J. (1987). The early development of low-birthweight infants: Relationship to health, family status, family context, family processes, and parenting. *International Journal of Behavioral Development, 10*(3), 301-318.

de Kieviet, J. F., Piek, J. P., Aarnoudse-Moens, C. S., & Oosterlaan, J. (2009). Motor development in very preterm and very low-birth-weight children from birth to adolescence: A meta-analysis. *Jama, 302*(20), 2235-2242.

Dean, R. S., & Davis, A. S. (2007). Relative risk of perinatal complications in common childhood disorders. *School Psychology Quarterly, 22*(1), 13.

du Plessis, A. J., & Volpe, J. J. (2002). Perinatal brain injury in the preterm and term newborn. *Current Opinion in Neurology, 15*(2), 151-157.

Favaro, A., Tenconi, E., Bosello, R., Degortes, D., & Santonastaso, P. (2011). Perinatal complications in unaffected sisters of anorexia nervosa patients: Testing a covariation model between genetic and environmental factors. *European Archives of Psychiatry and Clinical Neuroscience, 261*(6), 391-396.

Forsyth, J. K., Ellman, L. M., Tanskanen, A., Mustonen, U., Huttunen, M. O., Suvisaari, J., & Cannon, T. D. (2013). Genetic risk for schizophrenia, obstetric complications, and adolescent school outcome: Evidence for gene-environment interaction. *Schizophrenia Bulletin, 39*(5), 1067-1076.

Geldof, C. J. A., Van Wassenaer, A. G., De Kieviet, J. F., Kok, J. H., & Oosterlaan, J. (2012). Visual perception and visual-motor integration in very preterm and/or very low birth weight children: A meta-analysis. *Research in Developmental Disabilities, 33*(2), 726-736.

Golding, J., Emmett, P., Iles-Caven, Y., Steer, C., & Lingam, R. (2014). A review of environmental contributions to childhood motor skills. *Journal of Child Neurology, 29*(11), 1531-1547.

Grissmer, D., Grimm, K. J., Aiyer, S. M., Murrah, W. M., & Steele, J. S. (2010). Fine motor skills and early comprehension of the world: Two new school readiness indicators. *Developmental Psychology, 46*(5), 1008.

Jackson, D. B., & Beaver, K. M. (2013). The influence of neuropsychological deficits in early childhood on low self-control and misconduct through early adolescence. *Journal of Criminal Justice, 41*(4), 243-251.

Jaffee, S. R., Caspi, A., Moffitt, T. E., Dodge, K. A., Rutter, M., Taylor, A., & Tully, L. A. (2005). Nature× nurture: Genetic vulnerabilities interact with physical maltreatment to promote conduct problems. *Development and Psychopathology, 17*(1), 67-84.

Johnson, K. C., LaPrairie, J. L., Brennan, P. A., Stowe, Z. N., & Newport, D. J. (2012). Prenatal antipsychotic exposure and neuromotor performance during infancy: Prenatal antipsychotics and neuromotor performance. *Archives of General Psychiatry, 69*(8), 787-794.

Laucht, M., Esser, G., & Schmidt, M. H. (1997). Developmental outcome of infants born with biological and psychosocial risks. *Journal of Child Psychology and Psychiatry, 38*(7), 843-853.

Lundequist, A., Böhm, B., & Smedler, A. C. (2013). Individual neuropsychological profiles at age 5½ years in children born preterm in relation to medical risk factors. *Child Neuropsychology, 19*(3), 313-331.

McNeil, T. F., Cantor-Graae, E., & Weinberger, D. R. (2000). Relationship of obstetric complications and differences in size of brain structures in monozygotic twin pairs discordant for schizophrenia. *American Journal of Psychiatry, 157*(2), 203-212.

Meisels, S. J., Marsden, D. B., Wiske, M. S., & Henderson, L. W. (1997). *The Early Screening Inventory–Revised*. Ann Arbor, MI: Rebus.

Milberger, S., Biederman, J., Faraone, S. V., Guite, J., & Tsuang, M. T. (1997). Pregnancy, delivery and infancy complications and attention deficit hyperactivity disorder: Issues of gene-environment interaction. *Biological Psychiatry, 41*(1), 65-75.

Moffitt, T. E. (2005). The new look of behavioral genetics in developmental psychopathology: Gene-environment interplay in antisocial behaviors. *Psychological Bulletin, 131*(4), 533.

Pitcher, J. B., Schneider, L. A., Burns, N. R., Drysdale, J. L., Higgins, R. D., Ridding, M. C., ... & Robinson, J. S. (2012). Reduced corticomotor excitability and motor skills development in children born preterm. *The Journal of Physiology, 590*(22), 5827-5844.

Poole, K. L., Schmidt, L. A., Missiuna, C., Saigal, S., Boyle, M. H., & Van Lieshout, R. J. (2015). Motor coordination difficulties in extremely low birth weight survivors across four decades. *Journal of Developmental & Behavioral Pediatrics, 36*(7), 521-528.

Prechtl, H. (1968). Neurological findings in newborn infants after pre- and paranatal complications. In J. Jonxis, H. Vissern, & J. Trodstran (Eds.), *Aspects of prematurity and dysmaturity: nutricia symposium*. Leiden: Stenfert Kroese.

Raine, A. (2002). Biosocial studies of antisocial and violent behavior in children and adults: A review. *Journal of Abnormal Child Psychology, 30*(4), 311-326.

Raine, A., Brennan, P., & Mednick, S. A. (1997). Interaction between birth complications and early maternal rejection in predisposing individuals to adult violence: Specificity to serious, early-onset violence. *American Journal of Psychiatry, 154*(9), 1265-1271.

Raine, A., Reynolds, C., Venables, P. H., & Mednick, S. A. (1997). Biosocial bases of aggressive behavior in childhood. In A. Raine, P. A. Brennan, D. P. Farrington, & S. A. Mednick (Eds.), *Biosocial bases of violence* (pp. 107-126). New York: Plenum.

Seidman, L. J., Buka, S. L., Goldstein, J. M., Horton, N. J., Rieder, R. O., & Tsuang, M. T. (2000). The relationship of prenatal and perinatal complications to cognitive functioning at age 7 in the New England Cohorts of the National Collaborative Perinatal Project. *Schizophrenia Bulletin, 26*(2), 309.

Son, S. H., & Meisels, S. J. (2006). The relationship of young children's motor skills to later school achievement. *Merrill-Palmer Quarterly, 52*(4), 755-778.

Stanton, W. R., McGee, R., & Silva, A. (1991). Indices of perinatal complications, family background, child rearing, and health as predictors of early cognitive and motor development. *Pediatrics, 88*(5), 954-959.

Wichers, M. C., Purcell, S., Danckaerts, M., Derom, C., Derom, R., Vlietinck, R., & Van Os, J. (2002). Prenatal life and post-natal psychopathology: Evidence for negative gene-birth weight interaction. *Psychological Medicine, 32*(7), 1165-1174.

Wilson-Costello, D., Friedman, H., Minich, N., Fanaroff, A. A., & Hack, M. (2005). Improved survival rates with increased neurodevelopmental disability for extremely low birth weight infants in the 1990s. *Pediatrics, 115*(4), 997-1003.

Young, R., Riordan, V., & Stark, C. (2011). Perinatal and psychosocial circumstances associated with risk of attempted suicide, non-suicidal self-injury and psychiatric service use: A longitudinal study of young people. *BMC Public Health, 11*(1), 875.

Contributors

Dylan B. Jackson is an assistant professor in the Department of Criminal Justice at the University of Texas at San Antonio. His research focuses on the developmental precursors to antisocial and criminal behaviors, including factors related to child neuropsychological functioning and health.

Kevin M. Beaver is Judith Rich Harris Professor of Criminology in the College of Criminology and Criminal Justice at Florida State University and a visiting distinguished professor in the Center for Social and Humanities Research at King Abdulaziz University. His research is focused on the biosocial development of antisocial behaviors.

Perspectives on
Early Childhood Psychology and Education

PECPE publishes twice a year, in the fall and spring. These two special issues on specific topics are edited by one of the journal's associate editors, and also include a few general articles.

Editorial Policy and Submission Guidelines

Perspectives on Early Childhood Psychology and Education focuses on publishing original contributions from a broad range of psychological and educational perspectives relevant to infants, young children (to age 8 years), families, and caregivers. Manuscripts incorporating evidence-based research, theory, and practice within clinical, community, developmental, neurological, and school psychology perspectives are considered. In addition, the journal accepts test and book reviews, literature reviews, program descriptions and evaluations, clinical studies, and other professional materials of interest to psychologists and educators working with young children. Proposals for special focus topics may be made to the Editor.

Format: Manuscripts should be original work not currently submitted for publication to other journals. Authors must follow the guidelines of the Publication Manual of the American Psychological Association (Sixth Edition). Manuscripts may not exceed 35 double-spaced pages in length, including the cover page, abstract, references, tables and figures.

Submission: Submit an electronic copy of the manuscript for editorial review. Avoid including any identifying author information in the text. Selection of manuscripts is based on blind peer review. Include a cover page with the following information: the title of article, author(s) full name(s), title(s), institution or professional affiliations, and mailing and email address of primary author.

The cover page will not be sent to reviewers.

Selection Criteria:

• Importance of topic in early childhood psychology
  and education

• Theory and research related to content

• Contribution to professional practice in early childhood
  psychology and education

• Clear and concise writing

Submit manuscripts to the Editor at the following address:

Dr. Vincent C. Alfonso
Gonzaga University
School of Education
502 East Boone Avenue
Spokane, WA 99258

Email: PECPE@gonzaga.edu

CALL FOR PAPERS

Growing up poor: Negative sequelae on child development and beyond.

Poverty has direct effects on children as well as mediated effects in their development. This special focus of *Perspectives on Early Childhood Psychology and Education (PECPE)* invites manuscripts that explore the negative sequelae of poverty as it is related to impaired mental, emotional, and behavioral development; poor language and cognitive skills; limited academic achievement and educational attainment; as well as poor nutrition and health. Manuscripts should address the dynamic and developmental processes through which poverty operates. Although understanding the cumulative effects of poverty are important, how consequences at one stage in a child's development can hinder development at a later stage should be emphasized. Manuscripts should be original work not currently submitted for publication to other journals. Authors must follow the guidelines of the *Publication Manual of the American Psychological Association* (Sixth Edition). Manuscripts may not exceed 35 double-spaced pages in length, including the cover page, abstract, references, tables, and figures. Avoid including any identifying author information in the text. Selection of manuscripts is based on blind peer review. Include a cover page with the following information: the title of article, author(s) full name(s), title(s), institution or professional affiliations, and mailing and email address of primary author. The cover page will not be sent to reviewers. Submit an electronic copy of the manuscript for editorial review to Dr. Tammy Hughes, Associate Editor, PECPE: hughest@duq.edu.

General manuscripts for PECPE should follow the same format and submission guidelines except that they should be sent to Dr. Vincent C. Alfonso, Editor, PECPE: PECPE@gonzaga.edu or alfonso@gonzaga.edu by **January 31, 2017.**

Volume 1, Issue 2 of
Perspectives on Early Childhood Psychology and Education
was published in Fall 2016
by Pace University Press

Cover and Interior Design by Sara Yager
Cover and Interior Layout by Taylor Lear
The journal was typeset in Minion and Myriad
and printed by Lightning Source in La Vergne, Tennessee

Pace University Press

Director: Sherman Raskin
Associate Director: Manuela Soares
Marketing Manager: Patricia Hinds
Design Consultant: Sara Yager

Graduate Assistants: Taylor Lear and Rachel Diebel
Student Aide: Kelsey O'Brien-Enders

www.ingramcontent.com/pod-product-compliance
Lightning Source LLC
Chambersburg PA
CBHW071119280326
41935CB00010B/1061